Sluts

Trigger warning: this book discusses topics including sexual harassment, sexual assault, misogyny, transphobia, homophobia and other types of violence and discrimination.

Sluts

Beth Ashley

PENGUIN BOOKS

PENGUIN BOOKS

UK | USA | Canada | Ireland | Australia
India | New Zealand | South Africa

Penguin Books is part of the Penguin Random House group of companies
whose addresses can be found at global.penguinrandomhouse.com

www.penguin.co.uk
www.puffin.co.uk
www.ladybird.co.uk

First published 2024

001

Set in 10/17pt Sabon LT Pro
Typeset by Jouve (UK), Milton Keynes
Printed and bound in Great Britain by Clays Ltd, Elcograf S.p.A.

The authorized representative in the EEA is Penguin Random House Ireland,
Morrison Chambers, 32 Nassau Street, Dublin D02 YH68

A CIP catalogue record for this book is available from the British Library

ISBN: 978–0–241–67523–6

All correspondence to:
Penguin Books
Penguin Random House Children's
One Embassy Gardens, 8 Viaduct Gardens, London SW11 7BW

For Catherine, my favourite slut
(also my mother)

Contents

Introduction

I have always loved sex. Since the first time I ever experienced it – which you'll get to hear all about soon – I have been fascinated by it. Sex feels good. It gives me joy, pleasure and much-needed endorphins. Like many others, I want to enjoy that amazing feeling as much as possible.

Sometimes, my interest in sex is a nerdy one. As a sex and relationships journalist, I have made a career out of talking about sex, which is ironically less sexy than it sounds. It requires less actual sex (though at times it can inspire it) and more research, critical thinking and writing.

It can also involve a lot of travelling, speaking to people across the world about their own relationships with sex – the good, the bad, the ugly and the indifferent.

In Amsterdam, I watched ethical porn in a cinema with a bunch of other journalists. This type of porn aims to make sets safer places to work and seeks to change the way women are viewed in the industry by depicting female pleasure (and consent) on-screen. I have travelled to Negril in Jamaica to stay in a resort for swingers (people who enjoy group sex), becoming part of their lifestyle for a week. I visited Japan to discover their uniquely vibrant sex industry and how this intertwines with their culture.

Sex has provided me with an enormous amount of joy in my life. I have used sex to understand myself, to connect with people, to fall in love, to heal. Through casual sex I have learned about my body, how it works and how to make it tick. Through sex with ex-boyfriends who aren't in my life any more, I've discovered what feels pleasurable to me. And from all my sexual partners, including my husband, I have constructed my own personal value system, encompassing what I want from sex, what I'm interested in and what I actively don't enjoy.

Throughout my career, I've talked to people about their sex lives and connected deeply with those whom I have written about. I've investigated everything from why so many of us receive bad sex education to injuries caused by unregulated vibrators. I have interviewed, comforted and attempted to help those who are suffering with sexual dysfunctions, such as vaginismus (involuntary contractions in the vagina that make penetration more difficult) or issues producing erections. I've spoken to people whose partners have had countless affairs behind their back, as well as the people who can't stop having those affairs and don't know why. I've met gay men who have been slutshamed just for being gay, and women who have reported sexual assault and had their cases dismissed because of unrelated consensual sex they chose to have in the past.

These stories have impacted me greatly, and there's a theme that runs through every single one of them – an insidious problem at the heart of most of these people's experiences. It's something that burrows into our minds and sets up camp, affecting every aspect of our lives: slutshaming.

Slutshaming includes humiliating, embarrassing, insulting or otherwise bullying or harassing a girl or woman because of her sexual behaviour – or *perceived* sexual behaviour.

Sometimes slutshaming is simply calling someone a slut, which (according to all the dictionaries) is a woman or girl who is 'sexually promiscuous or considered to have loose sexual morals'. The word 'slut' has been a sexual slur for hundreds of years all around the world. It is often used to insult or degrade someone, along with its equally unfriendly synonyms: whore, hoe and sket, among many others.

Some people have reclaimed the word slut. This is similar to how 'queer' has been taken back and flipped into an empowering term for some people in the LGBTQ+ community. It has also happened to 'fat', with many people who are plus-sized wearing the word like a badge of honour.

There is immense power in taking ownership of language traditionally used against you. Many people see this as an act of strength, handing it back to the people who've been originally hurt by the words.

But it's important to note that not everyone is there yet. It's OK if you are not comfortable using 'queer' or happy to say you are 'fat'. And a lot of those who fit the description of 'slut' are not up for using that word either. This is totally understandable.

'Slut' is a difficult word for a lot of us. That's no surprise. It has heavy connotations and a painful history; it's loaded with stigma. Many of us don't want to use the word and feel committed to that stigma.

Reclaiming the word 'slut' isn't a recent thing. During the riot grrrl, feminist, punk rock movement of the early 1990s,

Introduction

Kathleen Hanna from the band Bikini Kill wrote 'SLUT' on her stomach in lipstick. Since then, feminists have attempted to regain control over the word and subvert its meaning. And we are seeing the impact of this today – there is the SlutWalk and the slut era trend (see Chapters Four and Seven), and there are slut meet-ups, slut workshops, slut pride campaigns and much more.

Yet many feminists, including Leora Tanenbaum, author of *Slut! Growing Up Female with a Bad Reputation*, argue that the reclamation is unhelpful. She explains that we live in a world where fraternities will hold a sign reading 'We Love Yale Sluts', and millions of us receive spam emails advertising the availability of 'Hot Local Sluts'. And as long as the term is being used in the traditional 'bad' sense – in these contexts, 'sluts' is referring to women as nothing more than sexual objects – and men are not in on the reclamation conversations and not using the term in the same way, Tanenbaum feels nothing has been achieved.

Personally, I want to reclaim the word. But it's easy to see both sides of this argument. That's why I've used both 'slut' and the term 'sexually free' interchangeably throughout this book. And I believe that if we shout it loud enough, the term could eventually become widely used in the *right* way.

For me and many others, taking back the word slut is a powerful, rebellious thing to do. It allows people to exercise freedom, release themselves from shame, cope with past trauma and celebrate their sexuality. To me, slut means 'I've had enough of the shame, and I'm doing what I want now.'

Whether you use it or not, you'll be welcome in sex-positive, anti-slutshaming spaces. But maybe try it on for size and see how you like it. You might be surprised.

Occasionally I will also use the word 'promiscuous' to describe sluts. I don't like this word but it's the one most researchers use when exploring this topic and we will be looking at a lot of these studies together.

While 'promiscuous' draws connotations of women who have casual sex with a lot of partners, this is not the only reason women are slutshamed.

Slutshaming can also include disrespecting someone for:

- Dressing in clothes that show skin, or clothes traditionally associated with sex work, such as fishnet tights, heels or animal print
- Flirting with people
- Having sexual feelings and/or exploring and openly exhibiting them
- Being friends with or associated with someone who is very sexual

- Having children young, or with different partners
- Engaging in specific sexual acts that are more niche or kinky

Slutshaming is everywhere. Painfully so. It's an experience almost every woman has had, and most marginalized people too. You might be among a group of friends or acquaintances when it happens. Or it might have happened at school when you were a kid. It might have happened in the workplace, even at home, or in public, when you were walking down the street.

Most people have their own story of slutshaming, and this book is going to interrogate exactly where slutshaming came from and how it impacts our day-to-day lives, whether that's at school or university, on dates, online, or in the workplace. We will also unpack how slutshaming influences our wider society, including justice and healthcare systems across the world. Though slutshaming might seem like no big deal to some, it has the potential to inflict serious harm.

According to 'Slut Shaming in Adolescence', a global study from the International Public, just under eighty per cent of people will be slutshamed at some point in their adolescence. It mostly happens to girls, but it is both boys and girls who do the shaming. Many teenage girls will see the word 'slut' online – either directed at them or someone else – by the time they are just twelve years old.

These statistics take on a whole new meaning, depending on who is being slutshamed. For women who are working class or queer like me, or women of colour, slutshaming becomes an entirely different, more complicated beast – something we'll also be exploring later in this book.

Over the last few years, sex positivity – a feminist movement encouraging positive, open, shame-free conversations about sex – has erupted into the mainstream. Sex scenes have started being depicted more realistically on TV and in film. The porn industry has been put under pressure to make significant changes to the way it looks on screen and the way it's created behind the scenes. Sex toys have started appearing in supermarkets, and new sex-related businesses have sprung up all over the place, ranging from apps to help with your sex life to sex party event organizers. The shift has signalled a cultural emphasis on female pleasure for the first time.

Despite the rise in popularity of sex positivity, it is still most people's default to shame sex. And shaming sex extends to shaming those who love it: the sluts, if you will.

This default shaming of sex impacts companies, including magazines and social media platforms. When editorial budgets are cut, the sex section is often the first to go. Social media algorithms are built to automatically investigate content that has a lot of flesh colour in it (assuming it to be a lot of skin showing) and to remove that content. Articles of mine have been taken down after publication because of backlash from groups who don't think I should teach people how to do certain sex acts safely. And, as I write this, thousands of sex education accounts are disappearing without warning from social media platforms thanks to new policies that mark *any* sexual content, educational or otherwise, as solicitation.

Slutshaming comes up in my personal life all the time, too. Recently, my husband and I were in a pub with my mum and her husband, enjoying a night out. I love talking to strangers and brought a few people I met outside to join us at our table. One of them – a man – started asking about my job. Usually, I can't talk about my accomplishments without feeling like I'm falling apart, but on this night I was feeling proud. Maybe it was the couple of whiskies I'd had, or perhaps the impostor syndrome forgot to switch itself on. But I spoke about my work happily, without dying inside.

I don't know if he somehow sensed that pride and wanted to murder it, or if he was simply speaking without thinking, but he turned to my husband, shrugged, and said, 'You've got your work cut out for you here, mate.'

I fell silent.

'Rather you than me,' he continued. And when I asked what he meant by this, he confirmed I was 'more than a handful'.

'More than a handful', 'brash', 'a bit much', 'a nightmare' – these are just some of the many ways people call a woman a slut without actually using the word. And they are terms I've heard since I've been physically able to hear. As a woman who has no issue with telling a man when he's being rude, and as an animated, excitable person who has massive boobs and loves showing them off when I go clubbing, there have always been people telling me I'm a slut. It's almost as if they're paid a salary to appear when I need them least and to humble me before I get too comfortable in my own skin.

As well as being slutshamed, I am also guilty of slutshaming other people. I slutshamed women I felt competitive with when I was a teenager. I slutshamed the girl I got cheated on with. I have slutshamed friends, myself, even my own mother.

Perhaps you have slutshamed someone, too?

In the eight years I've spent as a sex and relationships journalist, and now that I'm a good decade into my relationship with feminism, I've worked through my feelings about being slutshamed and slutshaming others, and reconciled myself with the word. I've gone from shaming myself for the things I enjoy to realizing it's OK to love sex, and lots of it. I've gone from fearing how people will perceive me and my sexuality to having joyful relationships with men and women (and those beyond the binary). I've gone from worrying about how I look to knowing that I shouldn't have to change the way I dress because of what people might call me.

I'm proud to be a slut.

And now, if I call my friends sluts, I mean it as a compliment. I know how much bravery and empowerment it takes to be a slut.

And my ultimate goal – for me, for you and for this book – is this: I want us all to work together to form a world where sex shame doesn't exist. I really believe we can do it.

I want you to look at your own sex life with self-love and admiration. I want you to look at your sexual history and think, 'Wow, I have lived!' I want you to consider your sexual experiences to be as culturally and personally enriching as being well-travelled or well-read. I want us to turn the 'walk of shame' into a walk of celebration.

And if you genuinely don't want to have a lot of sex, I want you to be proud of that without a shred of doubt, too. We should all be compassionate towards our sexual selves and shut down anyone who tries to make us feel shame about it.

I hope that by the end of this book you'll have a better idea of where slutshaming comes from and its impact, and that you will feel proud to be sexually expressive, whatever that looks like to you. I want you to have the confidence and knowledge to open up conversations that challenge slutshaming in your life and join me on an anti-slutshaming revolution.

1.

What is slutshaming?

I was fifteen the first time I was slutshamed properly. That time it felt different from when my friends would jab my ribs and call me a hoe for hitching my skirt up while walking past my crush. That was genuine support wrapped in schoolgirl banter. Even when I'd heard sexual rumours about myself at age thirteen, I was able to shrug it off and forget about it. But this incident really hit me.

In secondary school, I had a lot of friends, but the group I always hung out with was made up of boys: my boyfriend at the time and all his mates. We made the English department our meeting point before school started and during lunchtimes, and we would scurry under the stairs and sit there, usually watching YouTube videos or just passing the time by exchanging harmless banter.

As you can imagine, with ten of us sitting under some stairs, there wasn't a lot of room. We'd all end up pretty much sitting on top of each other. And one of the schoolteachers – who we'll call Miss Gillan – didn't like that.

'I'm sick of seeing you draped over boys with your shirt buttons undone every time I walk past you. You're obsessed with boys,' she spat at me. 'I'm going to have to call your mum and talk about your sexual behaviour at school.'

And then she said it. '*Slut.*'

Miss Gillan wasn't even my teacher and she knew nothing about me, but her words stuck with me from that moment. She made me feel as though I really was a slut and this was clearly how people had been looking at me all along. In fact, her words stayed with me throughout my teenage years and at times informed my sexual choices. I occasionally think about her to this day. Sometimes it's a revenge fantasy where I see her at the supermarket and trip her over, or she walks into a bookshop and sees that I've now built a successful career out of being a slut.

What is slutshaming?

That same year, one of the boys in that friendship group called me a dirty sket for reasons I don't even remember. I only recall the word and how it landed on my skin like a static shock. Some years later, another boy in that friendship group (not my boyfriend) sexually assaulted me. My teacher's comments were still swirling in my brain, leaving me wondering: would that have happened if I hadn't laid the groundwork to be sexually objectified? Should I have behaved differently to avoid this happening? Was being a sexual person what caused this? She, unjustly, made me believe it was my fault. It wasn't.

Little did Miss Gillan know, but I was already in the midst of the worst slutshaming of my life before she dropped the S-bomb on me. I didn't see it that way at the time, but I know it to be slutshaming now. A male relative I can't name had, unbeknown to me, set up spyware on my phone and computer and had been reading my messages for some time. As I mentioned, I had a boyfriend. There were sexts. There were nudes exchanged. There were detailed plans shared on exactly how we'd be 'losing our virginities' to one another (more on that later). I'm sure Miss Gillan would have disintegrated like a carbon pill in water if she'd seen them.

This relative printed those conversations out and handed them to my mum like he'd finished an important undercover assignment. He wanted her to condemn me. He wanted her to be ashamed of me for being sexual.

Thankfully, my mum made it clear that I had nothing to be ashamed of and that none of this was my fault. She introduced me to the concept of misogyny – meaning hate or prejudice towards women – and how it brings with it things such as slutshaming, sexist bullying and, in some cases, violence. She helped me see what slutshaming really is: sexual control. It's the process of embarrassing, insulting or belittling a girl or woman for her sexual behaviour to oppress her. It's a way of treating girls and women as sex objects instead of human beings, and ordering them to look, act and dress a certain way and to hide their sexuality.

Slutshaming can take many different forms. It's not always as obvious as outright name-calling, so we sometimes don't recognize it for what it truly is. But when we do understand it thoroughly, that's when we can challenge it.

The many faces of slutshaming

Slutshaming can look like a lot of different things, including:

- Calling someone a 'slut'
- Demeaning someone for wearing revealing clothes
- Spreading rumours about someone's sex life
- Criticizing someone for having sex
- Victim-blaming someone for a sexual assault
- Shaming someone for having a sexually transmitted infection (STI) and suggesting it's because of their sex life

- Blaming someone for the spreading of a nude photo of them
- Mocking someone else's sexual practices and preferences
- Assuming someone is dressing up just to please men
- Talking differently about girls who have sex than about guys who have sex

And it can include phrases like:

'I heard she slept with loads of people at a house party.'
'You should cover up.'
'She's like a man when it comes to sex.'

Each of these forms of slutshaming can have a significant impact on girls' and women's livelihoods, from restricting their freedom, enforcing secrecy around sex and discouraging them from speaking up about important topics like sexual assault to making them feel too ashamed to access sexual healthcare. We will explore the true dangers of slutshaming throughout this book and why it's therefore so important to fight it.

Slutshaming yourself

One of the most common effects of slutshaming is starting to shame yourself. A lot of people who've been slutshamed, or seen others be slutshamed, experience internalized slutshaming. This is where we police our sexual behaviour and make efforts to conceal it before anyone else notices.

It can look like:

- Shaming yourself for masturbation you enjoy
- Judging yourself, or thinking you're a bad person, because of sex you've had
- Thinking you shouldn't wear an outfit because it will look like you want sexual attention
- Feeling ashamed of your number of sexual partners
- Not wanting anyone to find out about elements of your sexual experiences
- Pretending you haven't had sex or masturbated when you have
- Distancing yourself from other women who've been accused of these things

Getting dress-coded

Like I did, a lot of people first run into slutshaming at school. A 2011 survey from the American Association of University Women found that slutshaming is one of the most common forms of sexual harassment that students in middle school and high school face in the USA. Around half of all girls experience it.

What is slutshaming?

Sex educator Jess Leigh, who works for British charities Bold Voices and Our Schools Now, which are both focused on ending sexual violence in schools, tells me it's something of an epidemic across the UK, too. In fact, just a quick scan of news headlines tells us it's a worldwide problem.

Back in 2014, schools in Utah, Florida and Oklahoma made headlines after telling young girls they couldn't wear short skirts because they'd be a distraction to the boys. The same year, a school in New York stopped more than one hundred girls who were wearing shorts from attending classes – even though it was the hottest day of the year – telling them, again, that their bodies would be a 'distraction'.

Showing how relentless this issue is, almost ten years later, in 2022, two schools in Australia were in the news for similar forms of slutshaming. One banned revealing clothing for girls in case they distracted male *teachers* (grim), and the other forced teenage girls to have their dresses for a school dance approved by teachers in advance, in case they were too short and 'distracting'. A school in the UK also made headlines after forcing girls to wear tights during a heatwave in 2023.

These codes target girls, sending the message that their physical appearance is to blame for how boys might behave towards them, and that covering their bodies is more important than their health, as they overheat for the sake of not looking slutty.

Some students have noticed these double standards around dress codes and taken action.

Those students from Utah, Florida and Oklahoma staged mass walkouts to protest about school slutshaming, boosting the hashtag #iammorethanadistraction online. The students in New York also protested by turning up to school in 'inappropriate clothing' every day until the school backed down and allowed shorts in the dress code. Absolute legends, if you ask me.

More recently, in 2021, a similar protest took place, when students in California opposed the banning of cropped tops and shirts in their school after being told they were a distraction to boys. Protesters wore cropped clothing and painted messages across their stomachs, reading, 'Distraction', 'It's not my fault' and 'Am I distracting?' – challenging the notion that their bare bellies disrupt classroom workflow.

The students also picketed, with signs saying, 'Teach boys to focus, not girls to cover up', and shared highlights of the protest on TikTok, with one student declaring on the platform, 'The dress code is sexist towards women and perpetuates rape culture. It makes us very uncomfortable.'

Asking for it

It's brilliant that young women are highlighting the connection between rape culture and slutshaming. Slutshaming can be something people brush off as a teenage non-issue, but, as we'll discover throughout this book, if it goes unchecked it can be very harmful.

Rape culture refers to the normalization of rape and sexual assault. When something happens frequently, even something as horrible as rape, we can start to accept it as part of our lives and play it down. One in three women across the globe will be raped at some point in their lifetime, which is a horrifyingly high number. Jess Leigh explains that slutshaming in schools ends up feeding rape culture, which we then carry into adulthood and 'the real world'.

Slutshaming dress codes perpetuate this problem. Think about it: if you grow up seeing girls and women vilified for wearing short skirts and accused of distracting boys and men with their bodies, watching them be slutshamed by both teachers and students, you could start to believe that girls and women are the problem. And once you believe that, you may also start to believe that boys and men would be justified if they acted violently towards girls and women.

Leigh notes that the term 'she's asking for it' is flooding schools across the globe. This is a common and horribly misogynistic response when a girl or woman is sexually attacked. We hear it a lot in the media.

One example is actress Emily Atack, who was told she was 'asking for it' by fans when she publicly shared her experiences of sexual harassment because she'd posed for glamour shoots for men's magazines in the past. Leigh explains that when schools set the idea that girls are a distraction if they don't dress a particular way, it teaches children that they are to blame if something terrible were to happen to them. That they, by wearing shorts on a boiling hot summer's day, or a short dress because they like the way it looks, are 'asking for it'.

This kind of slutshaming doesn't stop after school ends, though. It leaks into universities, too, where sixty-seven per cent of female students have been slutshamed and half of students have been sexually harassed or assaulted in the UK, along with around half of women in the USA and twenty-five per cent in Australia.

No schoolgirl should ever have educational time taken away from her because her skirt is too short or be told she's responsible for controlling boys' behaviour through her clothing. And no university student should ever be slutshamed for their clothing or their lifestyle. Nor is it ever their fault if they're assaulted, no matter what they're wearing.

Our Schools Now

The good news is that improvements are being made through a variety of grassroots campaigns and social enterprises. Leigh founded the organization Our Schools Now. In partnership with Our Streets Now, which combats street harassment, it consults with schools to raise awareness of the relationship between childhood slutshaming, dress codes that go overboard, and rape culture, in order to discourage educators from being part of the problem. As an organization, Our Schools Now also provides lesson plans and teaching materials, so the message is passed on to students.

Bold Voices

Bold Voices works hard on their mission to end all types of sexual violence in schools, which includes everything from slutshaming all the way to harassment and assault. On the Bold Voices website, there are comprehensive yet easy-to-follow plans of action for young people to end slutshaming in their schools, colleges and universities. You can download incredible stickers and posters with phrases like 'Not a distraction' and 'She did not ask for it', and learn tangible ways to communicate about slutshaming with your peers. They even have a template you can use if you want to email your school about your concerns over slutshaming and sexual harassment, and request action.

Our voices *do* matter and they *do* have an impact, as long as we allow ourselves to speak up.

Come on, don't be a prude

Though they may seem like opposites, prude-shaming is part of the same horribly problematic ideology as slutshaming. Prude-shaming is when girls and women are scrutinized or belittled for not having enough sex or not being comfortable talking about sex in social settings.

Like a lot of girls, I experienced both prude-shaming and slutshaming in school, from 2008 to 2013. I started getting slutshamed at fifteen, but prude-shaming came a couple of years before that, when I was ruthlessly bullied for being frigid. I remember feeling forced to have my first kiss with my boyfriend at thirteen years old in the school quad by a crowd of shouting prude-shamers who taunted that I 'wouldn't be able to do it' because I was 'too frigid'.

Then, once people started having sex, you had to have the right sex. You couldn't do it too much – that would make you a slut. But if you refused to do it at all? Well, then you were a prude! You must be good at sex, but you can't appear to enjoy it too much because that's slutty. You must like your body and not complain about it or hide it away, but you can't show it off too much because that's slutty too.

Sometimes it can feel like it's impossible to win. If you're not being slutshamed, you're prude-shamed instead.

It's like the character Allison says in the iconic John Hughes film *The Breakfast Club* (1985). When asked if she's ever had sex, she says it's a double-edged sword, explaining, 'Well, if you say you haven't, you're a prude. If you say you have, you're a slut.'

From a young age, women experience this sense that they can't win either way. They often feel they have to ultimately choose between being a prude or a slut. We see this all the time in the media. There were the early 2000s 'Are you a Megan Fox or a Lindsay Lohan?' quizzes in online magazines, where Megan was implied to be a 'slut' and Lindsay was depicted as the innocent girl next door. Teenagers were encouraged to find out which one they were. There was also the iconic (but unfortunately riddled with slutshaming) Taylor Swift music video for 'You Belong With Me', which saw 'slutty Taylor', who was conventionally sexy and wore revealing clothing, and 'virginal Taylor', who played in the school band and ultimately won the man's affections. The prevailing message: the virginal woman always wins. It's no wonder, then, given how often these messages are pushed in the media and appear all around us, that as kids we learn to accept this as 'just the way things are'.

When families slutshame

I often hear stories from girls and women about how their first experiences of slutshaming came from their own family members. In fact, the people we love the most can often be our biggest slutshamers.

Gina Martin, a British political activist and author, talks about this in her book *"No Offence, But ...": How to Have Difficult Conversations for Meaningful Change*. She explains that our family members have most likely experienced or seen slutshaming themselves and know all about its connection with rape culture, and so they slutshame us, thinking they are protecting us from it. That can look like telling us to cover up, because they think it will prevent us from being hurt by predatory people, or telling us we're 'acting like a slut' as a warning to avoid behaviour that could attract negative attention.

Even if it comes from a good place (and it is worth noting that it doesn't always come from a good place, even within families), the effects of being slutshamed by a family member are significant and can even tear families apart.

I spoke to twenty-eight-year-old Lindsey* (I have used pseudonyms for some of the people in this book, which I show using a * symbol) from Darwin, Australia, who told me she was kicked out of her home when she was seventeen years old because her family found out she was having sex, and they didn't believe in sex before marriage. She sofa-surfed around friends' houses and stayed with her boyfriend, and is only just starting to reconcile with her family now, eleven years later.

I also spoke to twenty-one-year-old Sophie* from Surrey, England, who told me that while she is in touch with her family, she hasn't lived with them since she was sixteen years old, instead opting to stay with her boyfriend and his family, because her mum frequently called her a 'tart' and a 'whore' for wearing revealing clothing.

And forty-three-year-old Jo* from Texas, USA, told me she has lost contact with over half of her family after they heard rumours she was having an affair and completely stopped speaking to her, rather than talking to her about it first.

Sex educator Erica Smith, who runs a programme to support people who were raised in hyper-religious, sex-negative environments, says she has seen this a lot among her own clients. 'Being rejected from your family or community due to your sexual behaviour is not uncommon,' she says.

When this happens, families are usually attempting to do a few things:

- Punish the person by cutting them off, giving them room to think about what they've done and rectify it

- Do what they believe is best for the person. Sometimes, people adhere so unquestioningly to the sexual morals they were taught that they are unable to see nuance. For them, everything is black or white; good or bad
- Distance themselves from their child's sexual behaviour so that they aren't seen as guilty by association. For example, Jehovah's Witnesses can be disfellowshipped for certain behaviours (including sexual sin)

No one is in charge of how you express your sexuality, even your family. If you're an adult who can consent to sexual activity, it's no one else's business how you choose to do that. And if you want to explore activities they would perhaps frown upon, it's OK to do that, as long as no one is getting hurt. It's also fine if you'd prefer to hide it from them, for your own sake.

It's important to note that our biological relatives are not the be-all and end-all when it comes to family. If you've been estranged, you can always find a chosen family. These are the people who you aren't related to, such as friends, who you choose to surround yourself with, and who still embrace, nurture, love and support you unconditionally.

You've been framed

Whether it's rumours spreading about someone using sex to advance their career, judgemental remarks about a colleague's living situation or love life, or comments on what someone is wearing, slutshaming happens a lot in office environments.

'I heard she fucked her way to the top.'

A New York University research paper, 'Slut-Shaming in the Workplace: Sexual Rumors & Hostile Environment Claims', found that many sexual rumours are spread in American workplaces. It also found that when official complaints were filed about offices being hostile environments, these usually involved unfair slutshaming.

In one case, an academic called Dr Jew spoke about the ten years of false rumours that were spread about her during her time at the University of Iowa. One of her colleagues told not only the staff but also the students that he'd seen Dr Jew having sex with the department head and that she was getting preferential treatment as a result. After months of receiving sexual slurs and having sexual cartoons posted of her around the workplace, she took the case to trial. Fortunately, it was found to be sexual harassment, but other similar trials haven't always reached this same result.

We also see this in the media all the time, especially in the political arena. In the UK in 2017, the *Daily Mail* newspaper slutshamed then prime minister Theresa May and then First Minister of Scotland Nicola Sturgeon for having their lower legs showing during political talks, printing a close-up photo on their cover. Australian Federal

Labor MP Emma Husar told *ABC News* that she quit politics because of slutshaming after *BuzzFeed* reported that she bragged about her sex life in the workplace and sexually harassed employees. Husar says that in the now-deleted article they called her 'a slut who boasts about who she has had sex with, which includes other members of parliament and members of her staff'.

'I guess slutshaming is the oldest trick in the book to bring down a woman. It's almost used as a method of torture,' she said in the interview.

One of the (many) awful things about slutshaming is, often, that the shame is based on guesses or lies about someone's sexual behaviour, rather than actual sexual behaviour they have engaged in.

This can look like:

- Spreading a sexual rumour about someone with no evidence about whether it's true or not
- Presuming someone to be promiscuous because of the way they dress, apply their make-up, or the tattoos they have
- Assuming a sexual partner will be interested in certain sex acts because they've heard a rumour that the other person has done it before

I like to call this 'slutframing' – get it? – because it's like slutshaming but you've been framed as well . . . You get it.

30

What is slutshaming?

There's little research that shows how many adults have been the target of a sexual rumour being spread about them. But for adolescents in Europe (between the ages of thirteen and seventeen), a whopping twenty-five per cent said they had been victims of sex-based rumours in just the six months preceding the Childnet International 'Young people's experiences of online sexual harassment: A cross-country report from Project deSHAME'. Given everything we know about how our experiences as teenagers influence our adult lives, I think it's safe to assume that these stats probably don't change too much among older generations.

Why do we slutshame people? This is a big question, and we're going to spend a lot of time getting to the bottom of it in this book.

Generally speaking, though, slutshaming is an attempt to belittle someone, often as a deflection from the shamer's own problems, or an attempt to increase their social value by bringing down someone else.

Erica Smith created the Purity Culture Dropout programme, which helps people who've grown up with slutshaming and had their sexual experiences affected by it, and she explains that, at its core, slutshaming is often about one-upping and reinforcing power imbalances. 'Often a person will slutshame someone because they think that person needs to be put in their place.'

She adds that slutshaming is sometimes also about jealousy. 'They may not be happy with their own sex lives and it's hard for them to see someone enjoying themselves freely.' Rather than get in on the sex positive action, some people find it easier to dismiss, belittle and even crush that positivity.

We learn to do this from a very young age, through social cues, pop culture and our learning environments (be it school, church or home). We will discuss the many ways that we can work towards building an anti-slutshaming culture in the world. One method Smith suggests is learning the art of calling out and calling in.

Calling out and calling in

As an example of calling out, one story in the news in 2019 concerned a female political adviser within the Australian government called Brittany Higgins who alleged that she had been raped in Parliament House, where the government meets. It is important to note here that the person Brittany Higgins accused later pleaded not guilty, was not convicted (a retrial was not sought after the first trial collapsed) and they strongly deny her claims.

Sue Hickey, a former member of parliament for Tasmania, later alleged that a senator (Eric Abetz) then made disturbing slutshaming comments about the incident. Hickey claims Abetz said to her, 'As for that Higgins girl, anyone that disgustingly drunk, who would sleep with anybody, would probably sleep with one of our spies and put the security of our nation at risk'. She made her allegations public in the Australian parliament while the session was being broadcast.

'Miss Higgins was raped. I accept that these are Abetz' views, but they are not shared by the wider community, who view these comments as slutshaming. No one, no matter how drunk or where they walk at night, deserves to be sexually assaulted. Even if she was drunk, a caring man would see that she got home safely,' Hickey said boldly in the session.

Abetz has categorically denied he made any slutshaming comments.

Regardless of whether Higgins' allegations were true, if Abetz had said what Hickey claims, it would have been shocking indeed, and demonstrative of how – even in a workplace as professional as the political arena – women are slutshamed. But Hickey demonstrated that calling out can be a great way to take the power back. I don't necessarily recommend calling someone out for alleged slutshaming behaviour in a parliamentary session on camera, since that can land you in some very hot legal water, but we can take what Hickey did and apply it to realistic styles of calling out in our own lives. We can borrow her bravery and tell the guy who keeps calling your female co-worker a slut in meetings to fuck off. In any professional working environment, it's so important for co-workers to defend vulnerable people when they are slutshamed.

Higgins is not the only woman to have been allegedly slutshamed in parliament. Another Australian senator, Sarah Hanson-Young, delivered an impassioned speech in the chambers when her colleague, Senator Barry O'Sullivan, told her she'd 'got a bit of Xenophon in her', referring to another male politician, Senator Nick Xenophon, and suggesting she had slept with him. In response, Hanson-Young stood up in the Australian parliament and called out every single politician in the room who she had ever heard make a slutshaming comment about another woman across all political parties and firmly told the prime minister that she would not stand for it any more.

What these women have done are perfect examples of 'calling out' executed well. And we can take inspiration from this to call out slutshaming behaviour that we witness and make our own schools, universities and workplaces free of shame.

Calling out

'Calling out' is about stopping people in their tracks when they say something wrong or offensive, and getting them to reconsider their words and actions.

Calling someone out can be scary because it's direct and confrontational, but it allows us to hit the 'pause' button when a harmful phrase or act is taking place and break the momentum. Calling out is best reserved for the moments when interruption is necessary to stop further harm from happening, when someone is clearly inflicting harm on purpose, and when we need to let someone know that their words are unacceptable and will not be tolerated by others.

When someone is slutshaming they might not know the weight of what they're saying, and sharing that context with them can help to end slutshaming, one person at a time.

You can call people out with phrases like:

- 'I don't find that funny. Tell me why that's funny to you.'
- 'It sounded like you said _____. Is that what you really meant?'
- 'I need to push back against that. I disagree. I don't see it that way.'
- 'I need you to know how your comment just impacted me/ someone else.'
- 'I feel obligated as your peer/colleague/co-worker/friend/ supervisor to tell you that your comment wasn't OK.'
- 'How do you know that this sexual rumour is true? Why are you telling other people this personal information?'
- 'I know you're annoyed with her but calling her a slut is irrelevant to the situation and sexist.'

Calling in

'Calling in' is better reserved for when you have a personal connection with the person doing wrong, such as a family member or a friend, or when it's clear that the person doesn't mean to be offensive or cruel and is simply misinformed. It's a gentler approach reserved for those you know will actively listen and make an effort to change. It helps when the person has previously demonstrated an openness and commitment to learning how to be better.

This can be done with phrases like:

- 'I'm curious. What was your intention when you said that?'
- 'I think someone else might interpret your words/actions differently. Imagine hearing your comment as a [insert group of people].'
- 'Why do you think that is the case? Why do you believe that to be true?'
- 'Is something making you nervous and that's why you're being this way? What can I do to help?'

Paying attention to slutshaming – where it happens, and who takes part in it – is the first step in eradicating it altogether. Once we do that, we can make it our mission to reject slutshaming in our lives and create an anti-slutshaming culture. We can follow anti-slutshaming practices in our schools and workplaces, and with our friends and family. These steps are how change happens, and we can all play a part in it.

2.

You don't owe anyone purity

The first time I ever had sex, I expected to transform, as though there would be this enchanting pumpkin-into-carriage moment. Or I thought I'd get some sort of recognition of reaching womanhood, like those letters people received from the Queen when they turned one hundred years old. But, just like most people probably find, my first experience of sex was unceremonious.

I was fifteen, as was my boyfriend Jon*, and we snuck into my house during the summer holidays to do the deed while my mum was at work. We'd started planning a week earlier, nervously buying condoms and lube from the pharmacy while panic-peeking over our shoulders like we were drug mules moving a shipment. His dad had given him condoms, but we were so shrouded in a specific embarrassment I couldn't name at the time, but which I now know is sex shame, that we avoided using them so his dad wouldn't notice one was missing.

We also agreed to not let anyone know at school, at least not for now, because of how the fallout would likely affect me. 'No one will care about you, but I'll get called a slag,' I remember telling him. He didn't argue back.

My older cousin, who doubled as my best friend, was in the year above me at school and was my go-to person for sex advice. 'Don't ever let the other girls at school find out if you touch yourself,' she told me once. And, 'Don't have sex with the popular boys, just your boyfriend, because they tell everyone.'

My school was also rife with lists. That might sound innocent at first, but they were a far cry from to-do lists. As I reached fourteen years old in the late 2000s, BBM (the messenger service for BlackBerry phones) was very popular. You could add people by username and easily broadcast messages to everyone in your contacts list. ASKfm and Formspring (two now-defunct platforms where you could broadcast anonymous messages to your network) were also taking off, and they were perfect for slutshaming.

You don't owe anyone purity

These platforms were the basis for sending lists of people and their behaviours or statuses or sexual preferences around my school. There was the 'dyke list', the 'big tits list', the 'slag list', the 'blowjob list' (I think this was supposed to be a list of girls who'd given them) and more. I'd already been on the dyke list and the big tits list. I didn't want to be on the slag list, nor did I want to make it on to ASKfm and Formspring lists, where sexual rumours spread stealthily and anonymously.

It wasn't that I didn't *want* to be having sex. I've known I was bisexual since that scene in *Aladdin* (1993) when Princess Jasmine gets kidnapped by Jafar and she's in *that* red outfit. This was reaffirmed by Velma's latex makeover in *Scooby Doo 2: Monsters Unleashed* (2004).

But because I was queer and too scared to come out, I pretended to be disinterested in relationships entirely. The late 2000s were not the most horrifically homophobic time – *Glee* (2009–2015) was running, after all – but there were still moments of old-fashioned homophobia sprinkled throughout my community, so I was too scared to be who I was or ask for what I wanted. I guess show tunes can't solve all the world's problems.

Secretly, though, I daydreamed about sex all the time. By the age of fifteen, I couldn't help but imagine what everyone at school would be like in bed while they were talking to me. I repeatedly replayed sex scenes from TV shows and films like *The Vampire Diaries* and *Blue*

Is the Warmest Colour (2013). I watched HBO's *Girls* (2012–17) and idolized how much the cast had sex and analysed their own sex lives with each other. I wanted sex and I wanted to talk about it with my sexy friends who had also had sex. I was basically an *aspiring* slut. I just didn't want any of the slutshaming I knew would come with it.

But when I met Jon I was so obsessed with him and attracted to him – he looked like a working man's Macklemore (an American rapper), only teenage and British (I guess that was my thing back then) – that the pros started to outweigh the cons.

So we had sex in my bed. And I was the exact same person afterwards. And I was confused about that.

He eventually went home and I glued the condom wrapper to a page in my diary because I'd seen Miley Cyrus do that in the film *LOL* (2012). 'We had sex,' I wrote very formally next to it.

The lack of difference was alarming to me. Why had nothing changed? I side-eyed mirrors all day to see if I could spot any of that 'post-sex glow' people always talked about on TV. I couldn't. Yet I still struggled to look directly at any family members just in case they could somehow tell what I'd done. Would they think I was a slut for having sex?

A year later, Jon ended our relationship and, because teenagers are extremely dramatic – especially ones who want to be writers when they grow up – I wrote an angry message on the same diary page where I'd glued our first of many condom wrappers.

'I wasted my first time. You really should wait as long as possible to lose your virginity because as soon as you do, you're tied together. And then he might leave you and you'll be broken forever.'

I'm disturbed looking back at my teenage diaries. Why was the idea that I could be left by the person I first had sex with so horrifying? Why did I expect that we should stay together forever once we'd had sex, even though we were just teenagers? Why did I feel used and damaged when he broke up with me for perfectly fair reasons, and he hadn't treated me badly at all?

At the time, these seemed like normal and justified feelings, but what teenage Beth was talking about were archaic concepts of virginity, soul ties and associating sex with loss – all staples of purity culture.

Purity culture, which we'll learn all about in this chapter, governs our society, setting the sexual rule book for women, and deciding who has value in society and who doesn't. It tells us what makes a good wife or girlfriend, or even just a good woman. And slutshaming is the tool that keeps women in check with those rules and regulations.

It's because of purity culture that we obsess over our 'first time'. But where do those ideas come from? And how can we shake them out of our brains?

Before we get into this, I want to start with one of the most important messages of this whole book, especially for my younger readers. It is always unequivocally your choice to decide when you are ready for sex. Every country has a legal age for consent. In the UK, it is sixteen. Of course that doesn't mean you *have* to have sex when you're sixteen. No one else gets to decide this for you. Listen to your body and mind, and only do what feels right for you.

A lady in the streets, a freak in the sheets

Most people grow up believing that virginity is something worth sealing away like a precious artefact. When someone takes it away from you, you're forever changed.

Depending on which country you live in and the culture you inhabit, the decision to 'lose your virginity' before marriage (when it's suddenly fine to have sex, apparently) can have serious implications.

This is, in part, down to purity culture. Originally a subculture within Christianity but now a phenomenon in wider society too, purity culture hinges on the idea that virginity is, well, *everything*.

You don't owe anyone purity

It's based on the notion that to abstain from sex is special, and even something to be worshipped. And this culture encourages deep criticism and judgement of anyone not making an effort to conserve their virginity for as long as possible.

Slutshaming has been around for a long time, since way before Christ (see Chapter Three). But the arrival of Christianity made it more widespread and framed slutshaming as a form of protection – as a way to keep people pure so God would be pleased with them. The entire culture, which saw a huge mainstream movement in the 1990s, particularly in the USA, was largely encouraged by members of authority within the Christian faith, such as pastors and priests.

Linda Kay Klein, author of *Pure: Inside the Evangelical Movement that Shamed a Generation of Young Women and How I Broke Free*, says that while the term 'purity culture' is generally associated with Christians, they are not the only people who carry those values. There are versions of purity culture within every religion. But it is by no means limited to religious groups. It is global and cross-cultural.

How do you get thousands of people to follow your rules about not having sex until marriage in the first place? Well, a lot of people fear being alone and not finding love, and that fear presents a perfect manipulation device. For this reason, a lot of sermons given in churches about staying pure (i.e. not having sex) were not only about pleasing God, they were also focused on attracting a man.

Purity culture's main message is: if you have sex before you're married, you will never find love, because no self-respecting man would want a woman who's already been penetrated by another man.

But purity culture even impacts those who have no relationship with religion or don't believe in marriage. There's a heavy religious influence in law and society even today, which means purity culture messaging has leaked into our collective subconscious. It affects how we date, how we speak about sex, and our views on what 'counts' as sex too. For example, many don't view certain queer sex acts as 'real sex' because they don't always involve penis-in-vagina penetration. It is the reason why so many people place such importance on virginity, and feel they have to keep their number of sexual partners low and have the 'correct' amount or type of sex, whether they're religious or not. Purity culture is not something we have to seek out – it finds us.

Outside of the church, messages from purity culture are everywhere, even in our psychology. The idea of 'good' and 'bad' women, and their sexual expression, is more commonly known as the Madonna-Whore Complex, an incredibly problematic theory. First discussed by Sigmund Freud (the creator of psychoanalysis, and a big old misogynist – booooo!), this complex explores the idea that male desire is sometimes flawed because, sexually, straight men are attracted to 'whores' (promiscuous women), but it's 'Madonnas' (homely, nurturing, 'pure' women) who they desire as life partners. Freud claimed that men with these conflicting desires could not love the whore, nor could they be sexually attracted to the Madonna.

This complex feeds into the media, and inevitably into almost all conversations around sex, from the classroom to school discos and beyond, leaving a lot of women feeling like they must impossibly master both sides. So they feel they have to curate an innocent, ladylike image of a perfect but sexless woman day-to-day, then take on the role of the sex-loving 'whore' for their husband behind closed doors, once married.

This attitude is highlighted by the phrase, 'a lady in the streets but a freak in the sheets'. Of course, this sets women up for failure straight away. How are we supposed to be brilliant in bed if we're not allowed to explore sex openly? But the idea was never about women succeeding. Instead, it's about control.

This misogynistic theory suggests that our sexual expression is not for us, but for our partners. It perpetuates the idea that our sexuality should be on lockdown until we're given permission to release it by a man. This is wrong. Your sexuality is entirely yours and you are the only commander of it. Ever.

Klein explains, 'In purity culture, gender expectations are based on a strict, stereotype-based binary. Men are expected to be strong, "masculine" leaders . . . [while] women are expected to support them – to be pretty, "feminine," sweet, supportive wives and mothers.'

Purity culture enforces those roles through placing sexual expectations on men *and* women. Technically, everyone is supposed to maintain absolute sexlessness before marriage (that means no sexual thoughts, feelings or actions). Upon marriage, they are expected to flip their sexuality on like a light switch, which can be very complicated to navigate for everyone involved.

All genders are victims of purity culture in a way, but Klein points out that the way men and women are controlled by it is very different. For men, it's about their minds. And for women, it's about their bodies.

'Men's thoughts and actions are said to be either pure or impure, while women *themselves* are said to be either pure or impure,' she says. 'Sexual metaphors often compare a "pure" woman to a brand-new shiny car while an "impure" woman is compared to a used car or bicycle that everyone around town has already driven and that isn't worth much any more.'

It's no surprise that, with such pervasive ideas about what makes a woman desirable, slutshaming is so rampant in society. As we explore further, it will become clear just how much purity culture has influenced our day-to-day lives, and the sex myths and messages it has left us with.

There's no science to purity culture

Categorizing women into 'virgins' and 'non-virgins' has long been a way to determine their value, creating a marketplace of 'good women' and 'bad women' for men. Under purity culture, virgin women are considered worthy of being married, and everyone else – whether they've had sex once or a thousand times – are sluts.

Gigi Engle, clinical sexologist, sex educator and author of *All the F*cking Mistakes: A Guide to Sex, Love, and Life*, explains that purity culture relies on three completely incorrect ideas about female anatomy and sexuality that are peddled as though they are facts.

Completely incorrect idea number one: The virginity myth

This is the idea that when you have sex for the first time your purity has been lost and you're now automatically categorized as a sexual being. Engle explains that sex is used as the 'ultimate moral compass' to decide who is pure and who isn't (the virgins being the purest of all). Words like 'virginity' are still used to describe a person's first experiences of sex; determining a woman's value by her sexual history still goes on today.

So, what actually happens to you when you lose your virginity? Nothing. Virginity is a social construct. You had sex. Good for you, bestie.

47

This myth has unfortunately persisted and plagued society. Even leading influencers in the sex-positive space and popular magazines will use words like 'loss' to describe a first sexual experience, which should only ever be a gain. They also use words like 'virginity', some as recently as 2023, despite most also publishing articles about virginity being a myth.

And while that may seem like innocent casual phrasing, repeating words like 'lost virginity' holds up these harmful myths that sex is something to be taken from you and leaves you changed forever.

Your first time having sex should be something to look forward to. Not something you ever have to fear. You should feel safe, happy and ready, and purity culture should not be allowed to take such an important moment away from us.

The idea of virginity also perpetuates harmful myths about sex in the LGBTQ+ community. Engle adds that because purity culture messages tell us that 'real sex' is a penis penetrating a vagina, those who have sex involving two vaginas or two penises can be left believing what they're having is not 'real sex'.

One study, 'Cherry Picking: Virginity Loss Definitions Among Gay and Straight Cisgender Men', even shows that many cisgender gay men consider penis-in-vagina penetrative sex to be indicative of 'virginity loss', despite them being unlikely to have it themselves.

You don't owe anyone purity

So let's get one thing abundantly clear: queer sex is absolutely, inarguably sex. So-called 'foreplay' is sex. You do not have to be entered by a penis to have experienced sex.

Making out can be sex. Dry humping can be sex. Masturbating is sex. Penetrative sex is sex. Only you can ever dictate what sex is for you.

Completely incorrect idea number two: The hymen myth

The hymen myth is the completely false idea that the hymen can be tested to determine whether a woman is a virgin.

Did you know that we know more about the surface of mars than we do about women's sexual anatomy?

Florence Schechter, biochemist, founder of the Vagina Museum in London, UK, and author of *V: An empowering celebration of the vulva and vagina*, tells me that purity culture myths manage to make their way into actual sex education textbooks and go unchecked (except by her and the museum, of course).

The sex education textbook *Review of Forensic Medicine & Toxicology*, used in universities in India, tells people how to spot the difference between virgins and non-virgins, and includes misinformation such as 'a true virgin will have an intact, rigid, inelastic hymen', who will take a finger into the vagina 'painfully', while a 'fake virgin' will have a 'loose, elastic and fleshy hymen' who 'easily admits fingers' into her vagina. It also says that fake virgins will have enlarged, dark nipples and a bigger clitoris, and their labia majora (the outer 'lips' of the vulva) will not be touching one another.

This information is, of course, simply untrue. Everyone's genitals look completely different, as do their nipples and other body parts. Our bodies may change over time due to age, illness or other factors, but they will not change from 'virginity loss' alone, and you will never be able to identify people who've had sex and people who haven't just by looking at their bodies.

Engle explains that virginity tests are sometimes done privately but are often ceremonial. Some take place during wedding ceremonies in particular cultures, and others have even been filmed and posted on TikTok!

In any case, a 'virginity test' involves inserting fingers (sometimes covered by a cloth) into the woman's vagina to determine whether her hymen breaks. If it does, she is determined to be a virgin and therefore 'pure'. If it doesn't, she is considered an 'impure' non-virgin and, depending on the culture and context, she may be subjected to abuse or even death. Engle explains that throughout history 'women have been known to cut between their toes on their wedding day so they can use the blood to pass the test if they know their hymen is already broken'.

Virginity tests have even been used and discussed openly by celebrities. In 2019, during an interview on the *Ladies Like Us* podcast, the famous rapper T.I. notoriously spoke about having his daughter's virginity tested annually to ensure she had not had sex.

He acknowledged a woman's hymen can be broken outside of sexual activity by things like cycling, athletics and horseriding, but countered this with: 'So, I say, "Look, Doc, she don't ride no horses, she don't ride no bike, she don't play no sports. Just check the hymen, please, and give me back my results expeditiously." '

Engle explains that the true purpose of the hymen is debated. A lack of research into women's anatomy and the sexual reproductive system means that there's very little thorough exploration of the hymen. But she says that the leading theory is that it's there to protect the juvenile vagina, keeping bacteria away from children while their immune systems fully develop. She can, however, confidently tell you what the hymen is not: a virginity indicator.

'For most women, the hymen breaks long before they even reach adolescence or puberty. You can lose it from stretching, horseback riding, bike riding, living, running, dancing – pretty much anything that involves lifting your legs,' Engle says. Even women who have had penetrative sex before could still have theirs intact. So as well as the numerous ethical problems involved with invasive investigations of a woman's hymen, it's also just a nonsensical strategy.

Bringing virginity tests to an end

Thanks to the tireless work of feminist speakers, campaigners, journalists, charities and the individuals who supported the cause, the World Health Organization (WHO) and the Royal College of Obstetricians and Gynaecologists (RCOG) officially declared virginity tests to be a human rights violation in 2014. They confirmed the tests have no scientific merit and that there is no known examination that can prove whether a woman has had vaginal intercourse.

This prompted several countries to make virginity testing illegal, and it was, in part, thanks to some of these key voices in the movement:

Sophia Smith Galer

Sophia Smith Galer is one of the leading journalists exposing virginity tests across the globe. She has also documented the impact of virginity tests in her book, *Losing It: Sex Education for the 21st Century*. Standing up to governments that allow virginity tests to continue has the power to inspire law change. We've seen it happen. And it also shares information publicly, meaning victims of virginity testing can understand that what they're going through is not OK and that there's something they can do about it.

Karma Nirvana

Karma Nirvana is an organization running the national Honour Based Abuse helpline in the UK. They are committed to ending 'honour-based' abuse, which includes virginity testing, and they offer training to professionals in educational, judicial and healthcare environments so they can spot the signs when virginity testing might be taking place. Karma Nirvana also gathers data to inform policies, services and campaigns for change. Previously, they campaigned relentlessly in the UK to ban virginity tests, which were being carried out in various areas around the country.

Following Sophia and Karma Nirvana's work, among many others, the UK government has made virginity testing or hymenoplasty illegal as of 2022. Following suit, virginity testing is also now illegal in India as of 2023.

This is a great example of how individual and organizational campaigning can be so powerful. We're all able to be the change that happens in the world, and I believe we can end virginity testing (and other slutshaming practices) in every country across the globe by continuing these efforts.

This obsession with virginity, and the consequences it has, is why many modern sex educators today use the phrases 'first time', 'first sex', 'sexual debut' or 'sexual initiation'. Simply changing how we talk about our first time, and the specific language we use, has the power to change cultural norms.

Dating, waiting and mating

Purity culture has also entangled dating with ideas of sexual purity. Yep, you won't just find purity messaging in churches. It may also find you in your personal conversations about dating, on your next blind date or even on Hinge.

Before twenty-eight-year-old marketing assistant Hannah*, from New York, USA, even knew what sex was, she made a promise to abstain from it. On her eleventh birthday, she was given a purity ring by her parents. She tells me her father revealed it 'proudly, like he was announcing a promotion', and then he slid it on to her finger while down on one knee, as if he was proposing.

Hannah's family wanted her to keep her virginity until she was married, like a 'good Christian girl', and her wearing this ring was a symbol of her acceptance. 'I was mostly just excited to be getting pretty jewellery. I was a kid after all,' she says.

Hannah was told that it was important to keep her virginity, so that it wouldn't be ruined before she met her husband. She said she was always unsure exactly *how* having sex would ruin her, but that it had been made clear during conversations at home and at her church, where she went every Sunday, that premarital sex was an abomination.

At the time, Hannah felt like she had an important mission to uphold. She had to protect her virginity until marriage, and this would help her get into heaven one day.

Purity rings (also known as promise rings or abstinence rings) are a purity culture staple worn as a promise of chastity – the practice of refraining from sex before marriage or, in some more extreme cases, all sexual intercourse forever. Many people also make these pledges without a ring, with thirty-two-year-old Melissa telling me she signed a certificate promising to keep her virginity in a church in Dudley, UK, when she was just thirteen years old.

These rings have been knocking around for a long time. They first popped up in the 1900s in Christian organizations in the USA, particularly in Catholic and evangelical Christian groups, who wanted more people to pledge their commitment to virginity.

These groups used phrases like 'True Love Waits' and 'Silver Ring Thing' to promote purity, and package the rings as an honour, and make it a fun community to be part of. After all, when you're a kid, who doesn't want to be involved in a trend that involves fun catchphrases and wearing jewellery with pals?

It wasn't until Hannah was fourteen that she realized what her family had truly signed her up for and what she'd agreed to do. She wanted to start kissing boys and potentially sleep with them too, but whenever she felt those urges she would look down at her ring and tell herself off. And it wasn't even the abstinence that mattered to her – most of all, she didn't want to upset her parents.

Celebrity celibacy

If you're of a certain age and you were knocking around at any point during 2008 to 2012, you'll likely have heard about purity rings in association with the Jonas Brothers.

For the unacquainted, the Jonas Brothers are an American pop-rock band who formed in 2005 and gained a huge teenage fanbase due to their appearances on the Disney Channel. And they wore purity rings. Which they talked about. A lot.

It all started when they were spotted at a press event wearing matching rings, with many fans presuming them to be married rather young. The brothers soon confirmed they were wearing purity rings, and they were wearing them as a promise to abstain from sex until marriage. But when they broke up in 2013 (a dark day for most teenage girls), their purity rings disappeared, along with their music.

During a 2022 interview on *The Late Late Show with James Corden*, the brothers shared the truth – the purity rings were part of an orchestrated wholesome family-friendly image constructed by Disney. And it worked. That squeaky clean, godly image sold records and soon other celebrities like Miley Cyrus, Jordin Sparks, Selena Gomez and Demi Lovato followed suit with their own purity rings. These celebrities, in a way, became icons of purity culture. In fact, within three months of the brothers talking about their rings, sales of purity rings had increased by 113 per cent.

Along with being unethical, especially when they are forced, virginity pledges are also counter-productive. They literally do not work. A study from the University of Massachusetts found that purity rings pretty much mean nothing because girls who wear them are almost twice as likely to get pregnant.

The study found thirty per cent of people who pledged abstinence become pregnant outside of marriage within six years of breaking that pledge, while eighteen per cent of people who did not promise abstinence become pregnant outside of marriage within six years after first having sex.

It also showed that people who make promises to wait to have sex until marriage are incredibly likely to break those pledges.

What's more, those who pledge abstinence – ring or no ring – are less likely to be educated about sex, as sex education is typically avoided through fear of temptation. So, not only are people wearing purity rings still likely to have sex, but they are then more likely to become pregnant than their peers who made no such promise, because of a lack of education!

The ideas of sexual control within dating have transferred from religion into wider society. It's not only daters within the Christian faith who are controlled by these 'rules'. It's something I've seen in my friends, time after time. One of my best friends was asked for her 'magic number' (the number of people she'd slept with, sometimes referred to as a 'body count') on a first date. When she answered, he applauded her for having a low number, telling her she was 'one of the good girls' – as though she was a Border Collie, and not my amazing, complex and interesting friend who's worth far more than the number of people she has slept with. And she's not alone – just under half of all men and women have been asked by their current romantic partner what their own 'body count' is as part of the dating process. We've been brought up to believe that a partner's sexual history will impact their ability to love us. It won't.

Completely incorrect idea number three: The 'soul ties' myth

Now feels like a good time to discuss a third completely incorrect idea that purity culture relies on: that with each sexual partner, parts of our soul have been exchanged. This reinforces the idea that there is just one person (well, man – purity culture completely erases homosexuality) out there for every woman. It tells us that we must keep ourselves pure until we find him, and when we do eventually fall in love with our one partner, get married and have sex with him, our souls will be tied forever and ever.

Engle tells me that soul ties were invented to make women feel guilty for having more than just one sexual partner. Purity culture scares us into believing we'll lose any chance of finding a partner – the person whose soul will be tied with ours forever – by sleeping around.

So what actually happens when you have sex with multiple people? Nothing. You just have sex with multiple people. PS There is no scientific evidence whatsoever to support the existence of the soul in the first place, so there's certainly no need to worry about it breaking off with each sex session.

Even if you don't believe in God or soul ties, this idea can still leak into your perception of sex and relationships. It's the reason I felt like I was tethered to Jon forever once we had sex and that I'd wasted my virginity when he broke up with me. It's the reason there are, at the time of writing, 437.4 million views on TikTok videos about soul ties, spreading misinformation about what happens to our souls, bodies and psyches after a break-up. Many of these videos revolve around advising people to be 'more selective about sexual partners', claiming the body has forever been impacted once you've had sex with someone.

Engle tells me how influencers use these myths to sell products like cleansing balms, yoni steaming devices (an age-old natural remedy said to cleanse the vagina and uterus by sitting naked over a pot of hot water) or sage (to burn near the vagina – which can be seriously dangerous) while telling you to 'put yourself first' and 'expel the negative energy of men from your body so it doesn't harm your future relationships'.

From around 2020 to 2023, 'soul ties' started being used casually, particularly on social media, to describe an instant and unexplainable connection with a person. *Women's Health* magazine described it as 'the phenomenon of meeting someone for the first time and feeling like you already know them' in an article exploring the term. While this might seem romantic, it's still connected to purity culture ideas of searching for permanency and being bound to the people we have sex with.

Sticky tape sex ed

So why is there still such an obsession with virginity and abstinence?

It's easy to point the finger of blame solely at religion, but that wouldn't be fair.

You don't owe anyone purity

Religious practices around purity of course seem extreme, and there's going to be a natural temptation for people who are not religious to place blame on those who are, and consider themselves separate from this whole culture.

But the themes of sex shame, gender roles and virginity are a deeply embedded part of our world, and we can't work as a collective to challenge these damaging ideas if we're pointing fingers at certain groups of people.

So where else do we learn these harmful ideas? Well, if there's anything that unites us all, it's that most of us had terrible sex education lessons at school.

In the UK, a 2023 survey from the Sex Education Forum, a charity who promote and protect the health of young people by improving sex education, shows that most teenagers are unhappy with the sex education they receive at school and feel they're not being taught enough, adding that they want to be taught information about 'real life' sex.

In Japan, forty per cent of teenagers are dissatisfied with the sexual education they receive. In fact, across the whole of Asia, according to Atlantis Press, sex is an 'unspoken taboo' and a 'controversial subject', so the sex education is generally falling behind.

In mainland Europe, a similar story is told: according to the European Union's annual review, students are not learning enough about navigating sex and relationships, with only one in ten teachers feeling like they were sufficiently trained to deliver the information.

In the USA, it seems only the opinions of American parents – not the students – are taken into consideration regarding sex education, which inevitably has an impact on the content being taught.

And as for Australia, ninety-eight per cent of teenagers want sex education and feel it's important, but only 24.8 per cent said their most recent sex education lesson was relevant to them.

Across the globe, young people are receiving inadequate sex education, and purity culture is finding its way into curriculums in various countries too.

In 2023, an episode of the investigative series *Four Corners*, aired on Australia's ABC Television channel, reported that a lot of schools were using the 'sticky tape' technique to teach children about abstinence. This practice involves passing sticky tape around a classroom, encouraging pupils to press it on their desk and pass it along to the next child. By the time the tape has reached every class member, it's dirty and unusable. That, according to this lesson, is representative of a woman who has casual sex.

You don't owe anyone purity

Erica Smith says these experiences are common in schools across the whole world, especially in the USA. A 2020 study from the Guttmacher Institute, a leading research and policy organization committed to advancing sexual and reproductive health and rights in the USA, showed twenty-eight US states have made abstinence-only sex education mandatory. This is where children are discouraged from having sex instead of being taught how to do it safely. In comparison, only nine states instruct teachers to emphasize consent. Some states don't require sex education at all. Shockingly, only nineteen states in the USA even require sex education to be medically accurate, which explains why so much misinformation about female anatomy ends up printed in textbooks and absorbed into our brains.

In the USA, abstinence-only education received at least $15 million in federal support in 2015, and the lessons usually come with a lot of shame-based practices. Smith tells me that a common method for teaching abstinence involves children watching as a delicate flower is mercilessly crushed or its petals are plucked in front of the whole class. Then the teacher will tell young girls that this – the crushed, dirty flower, losing its petals and holding on for dear life – is what becomes of them when they have sex. The more they have sex, the more dirty, used, damaged and unwanted they'll appear to others.

This method is used in the Choosing the Best book series, which includes *Choosing the Best Path* and *Choosing the Best Journey*, according to the Sexuality Information and Education Council of the USA. These books are a curriculum for teaching abstinence. This practice is so common, in fact, that it features heavily in the popular Netflix series *Jane the Virgin* (2014–19), where the main character, Jane, becomes obsessed with holding on to her 'virginity' after her grandmother used the crushed-flower technique to sway her away from sex before marriage. She even frames the damaged rose and displays it above her bed as a reminder of what could happen if she has sex.

Abstinence-only sex education is usually justified by arguments stating that it will reduce teen pregnancies and STIs. Yet Erica Smith explains that often this type of sex education in schools doesn't cover contraception, consent or any kind of information around communication within sex, meaning the chances of it actually reducing these things is highly unlikely. In fact, along with an increased rate of pregnancy in these schools, STI rates are also going up, since people who are expected to remain abstinent don't know how to practise safe sex when they do eventually choose to have it.

Despite these findings, many parents still want their children to learn this way. One study shows eighty-one per cent of adults in the USA believe their children should be taught abstinence-based sex education 'alongside other [pregnancy and STI] prevention methods', and a whopping thirty-one per cent believe children and teenagers should only be taught abstinence, despite overwhelming evidence that it doesn't work the way they think it will. If this isn't purity culture in action, I don't know what is.

When British people were asked to identify the best kinds of relationships to them, in the National survey of sexual attitudes and lifestyles 2003, forty-eight per cent of women and just over forty per cent of men said 'married, with no other previous sexual partners' would be best. It's clear that by allowing purity culture to filter through our education, we end up carrying those myths into our adult lives too.

Purity culture being taught in schools is dehumanizing. Children and teenagers deserve an education that offers objective, practical, sensitive and scientifically backed advice for navigating sexual relationships.

Many sex education experts across the globe, including the likes of the Sex Education Forum in the UK, agree that consent should be at the centre of sex education classes in schools, colleges and universities. And I agree. As long as everyone involved in sex is safe, of consenting age and wants to be there, it's no one's business what happens between them.

Thankfully, there are a number of organizations, grassroots campaigns and charities working hard to take purity culture out of schools and to get sex education classes where we need them to be.

Anti-purity culture sex educators

There are a number of independent sex educators out there in the world truly making a difference to sex education both inside schools, universities and educational environments, and in one-to-one sessions. I'm very happy to say that there are so many of these brilliant sex educators that I cannot name all of them. That would be a book of its own. But here are some examples of a few and the important work they are doing:

My Body & Yours

My Body & Yours, run by founder and independent sex educator Laura Clarke, offers sex education classes to various schools in the UK and makes a conscious effort to teach students about their bodies, how to navigate romantic and sexual relationships, and includes lessons on important subjects like understanding consent.

The Purity Culture Dropout Program

If you have been raised in a purity culture environment and you want to learn about sex without that influence, Erica Smith's Purity Culture Dropout Program is designed for exactly this. She works with clients across the USA.

She also hosts an array of workshops available to everyone across the globe, including how to have sex for the first time and enjoy yourself, and how to let go of purity culture's values and focus on your own.

You don't owe anyone purity

Smith is also very vocal on her social media platforms, alerting people to the ways purity culture hides in plain sight and influences our sex lives in a range of environments.

Brook Sexual Health Services

Part of the National Health Service in the UK, Brook Sexual Health Services is a charity that regularly works with doctors, researchers and independent consultants from a variety of diverse backgrounds to improve sex education and ensure it's free from purity culture messages.

In addition to these changemakers, new legislation is paving the way for better, more consent-focused sex education in a variety of countries. In the UK, Canada, Australia, New Zealand and some countries within the European Union, it's now a legal requirement to offer sex education in schools that includes lessons in consent.

Meanwhile, the American Pediatric Society has officially released a statement to say they do not recommend abstinence. The World Health Organization has endorsed consent-focused comprehensive sex education and has recommended that purity culture-based programmes such as abstinence-only education are no longer used. It's both comforting and liberating to know there are so many sex educators and policymakers undoing purity culture's dirty work, both in schools and in adulthood.

I want to end this chapter by reassuring you that no matter your age or background, it's never too late to unlearn purity culture. We are all able to undo its shackles at any time. It's just about finding the right people and the resources that prioritize science, safety and pleasure over false morality.

And remember: virginity is a construct. It always has been and will continue to be nothing more than that. Whether you've had sex once, or you've had sex with lots of people; whether you're thinking of having it soon, or it's not for you – your choices will not change who you are as a person. You don't owe anyone purity, not your Hinge match, your mum and dad, your mates or your teacher. *Especially* not your teacher.

3.

The true history of sluts

It's 1632, and one of the most iconic, complex and powerful characters in history lies dying of both breast and uterine cancer. Frances Carr, Countess of Somerset, at this point, is an English noblewoman best known for being a central figure in the murder of Sir Thomas Overbury. In fact, she was found guilty but later spared execution and released from the Tower of London once new evidence that proved her innocence was discovered.

Carr was also one of only a few women in that period in the UK who was able to get a divorce. Well, she received an annulment (like a divorce, but instead the marriage is declared null and void) after her first marriage, which she entered at thirteen years old, inevitably went nowhere. The marriage had been more of a business transaction, as many were back then, and she eventually fell in love with someone else. Still, the annulment was a pretty impressive feat, considering Henry VIII had only invented divorce a few hundred years earlier and they were almost always granted to men.

Even though we've only begun to scratch the surface of her life, it's clear Carr lived colourfully and loudly. Her young marriage, made to form a political alliance, her falling in love with Robert Carr, her wrongful conviction and eventual release, her duties as a countess. Her *life*. None of this is recognized in her death record.

Instead, her local minister, Arthur Wilson, recorded that Carr was 'killed by a disease of the below parts' and 'that part of her body which had been the receptacle of most her sin grown rotten (though she never had but one child) the ligaments falling, it fell down and was cut away in flakes, with a most nauseous and putrid savour which, to argument, she would roll herself in her own ordure in her bed, took delight in it.'

In layman's terms, this minister saw a powerful, confident and intelligent woman taking her last breaths and chose to slutshame her, recording that her body was rotting directly because of her sinful sex life (i.e. being a slut), and he even suggested that she was turned on by the pain inside her body.

It's one of the most heinous examples of slutshaming in history.

The monarch at the time, James I (who was, for the record, a big slut), was described as a man of 'sexual excess' demonstrated in his many 'illegitimate' children. As a result, during his reign, there was far less emphasis on noble or royal people needing to appear pure. This even extended to women for a short time, with upper-class women, including members of the monarchy, wearing more cleavage-friendly dresses, some that even showed their areolas. And the sexual tone of courting (that's 'dating' in olden-times lingo) completely changed too, with much more open sexual expression and flirting. There was also less sexual denial during this time. People didn't conceal their sex lives like they had before and weren't preaching sexual morality to one another as often.

But women's sex lives were still heavily judged behind the scenes. It was hard for people to let go of the gender roles and sexual standards they'd previously been conditioned to have, so many still frowned upon those women who were starting to sexually express themselves in public or one-on-one with people they were into.

And as we can tell from Carr's death record (and the societal slutshaming we still face today), that brief era of freedom was short-lived.

Something all women have in common, throughout history, is the policing of their sexuality. For this reason, slutshaming is all around us – in our history books, schools and homes. It leaks, like toxic oil, into our media and conversations, even in the most sex-positive of spaces. Someone, out there in the world, is probably getting slutshamed right now.

It didn't start with Frances Carr and it certainly didn't end there. In fact, the reason this chapter is called 'The *True* History of Sluts' is because so many iconic women in history have had their legacy warped because people didn't agree with their sexual expression.

The question of where slutshaming comes from is hard to answer, as it depends on so many factors, including who you're talking to and which country you're talking about. There are a lot of theories as to who invented slutshaming, how it happened and why, and it's something historians continue to argue about. Most historical records have also been kept by men, which changes the lens of how we understand women in history.

In order to change the way our systems work and to fight the slutshaming that still exists today, we have to look back and understand how we got here in the first place.

So, where did slutshaming *really* come from?

Inventing the patriarchy

To unpack the origin of slutshaming, we have to start with the invention of patriarchy. Personally, my least favourite invention. Shortly followed by low-rise jeans and spam emails.

Patriarchy is a system where men hold the positions of power and privilege in society, and women are excluded. We live in a patriarchal society right now, which is why women typically earn less money than men and, as multiple studies have shown, are less likely to be taken seriously in professional, educational, medical and even dating environments. For example, doctors are more likely to misdiagnose women with an illness, or completely miss a diagnosis in the first place.

There are two main theories about how patriarchy was created – Engels' theory and Marxist feminist theory.

German philosopher, historian and political theorist Friedrich Engels (1820–1895) had a theory that patriarchy was invented to enforce capitalism, which is the name for the economic system in which private individuals own and run companies, and the profits flow to those at the top.

Before the Industrial Revolution (roughly 1750–1900), when many factories and other workspaces were built, a lot of men worked from home, such as blacksmiths, carpenters and bakers. Being at home meant that their wives would help them out. So, despite

73

popular belief, loads of women worked during this period. In fact, the female unemployment rate is higher in 2023 than it was in Victorian times. (We often hear that historically women have been housewives, but this was only true of wealthy women, making this just one of many examples of class erasure in our history.)

When men stopped working from home and began working on-site, this changed the way women worked. Engels' theory was that this was the beginning of gender roles. The wives were no longer helping their husbands with their trades and so they were expected to start doing more at home, which is where the idea of the housewife came into play.

Because of gender roles (see Chapter Five), we reached a point where men were doing all the off-site labour and women were essentially just birthing an endless stream of children. Engels believed that this was how patriarchy was created.

On the other hand, Marxist feminism, which is an extension of the theories of German philosopher and economist Karl Marx (1818–1883), argues that patriarchy was created much earlier, with the invention of agriculture.

Before the agricultural revolution around 10,000 years ago, we were hunter-gatherers, and that was our main way of obtaining food. The story goes that the males did the hunting and the females did the gathering. But Florence Schechter explains that whether women hunted actually depended on what was being targeted. She notes that if animals were quite easy to catch, then women would hunt for them too. Women had babies to look after and so they wouldn't waste time hunting an animal they couldn't catch easily, and would gather food instead. The males, however, did not have the responsibility of looking after babies and were able to hunt much more than women.

During this period, men and women were actually far more cooperative in balancing the workload than we're often led to believe. Yet, this dynamic changed with the invention of agriculture. We went from gathering and hunting to being able to grow crops and store food like grain for the whole winter.

Hoarding grain meant that for the first time people could accumulate wealth. People worked really hard all year round to grow and store their grain. And then there became an issue of inheritance. The men who had worked on their grain supply wanted to make sure that their wealth was only being shared among people that they were related to.

This is where slutshaming comes in, and it comes in hot.

Schechter explains, 'Basically males were like, "How can I make sure that my wealth is going to go to my biological children?" And therein the patriarchy was created, as a means to ensure paternity certainty.'

Essentially, with both Engels' and Marx's theories, the only way that men could be certain their children were definitely theirs was if their wives were stuck in the house with no jobs to do other than housewife chores and baby duties, ensuring they had no opportunities to sleep around. Eventually, this developed into the idea of policing women's sexuality directly. If a woman appeared to be a slut, a man could not trust her with paternity certainty and that would threaten his wealth.

This is where valuing 'virginity' came into play outside of religion. 'If a woman was a virgin before marriage, men could guarantee that any baby she has is definitely theirs,' Schechter says.

So, to make sure their partners were not sleeping around, men would go to great lengths to control their wives' behaviour and thereby guarantee that their wealth wouldn't be used on another man's child.

Are you married or are you a sex worker?

A lot of historians trace the origins of slutshaming back even earlier, arguing that the Ancient Romans, whose empire spanned across Europe, northern Africa and parts of the Middle East, are to blame.

The true history of sluts

In the Roman Republic, you could differentiate between married women and sex workers (then referred to as 'prostitutes') by their clothing.

Now, I know what you're thinking. There are more kinds of women than just 'married woman' and 'sex worker', right? Not to the Romans, unfortunately. According to medieval historian Dr Eleanor Janega from The London School of Economics and Political Science, any woman who was a slut, i.e. enjoyed sex outside of marriage, was considered a sex worker. To the Romans, this translated to being an unmarriable peasant and, well, disgusting. Because of this, it's actually very likely that women who have been recorded as sex workers in history may have merely been having sex outside of marriage.

So, the Romans popped married women in stolas, which were long, pleated, sleeveless robes, while sex workers wore togas, which looked a bit like white skater dresses worn on one shoulder.

It wasn't just sex workers who were slutshamed, though. Married Roman women competed to be seen as 'the most sexually virtuous' wife. They were punished or censured for appearing overly sexualized, for enjoying sex, for talking about sex with other people or being found to have had premarital sex.

Ancient Roman philosophers, including Cicero and Saint Augustine (also known as Augustine of Hippo), had a lot to say about sluts. It seems that all the male great thinkers of history did. Cicero warned men to watch out for women, and 'not just her flashing eyes (*flagrantia oculorum*) and loose language (*libertate sermonum*) but her hugs, her kisses, her beach parties, her boat trips, her carousels that make her seem not only a prostitute but a prostitute who solicits men shamelessly (*proterva meretrix procax*)'. (Personally I love the sound of this woman . . .)

This is when Ancient Rome started embracing the arrival of Christianity, meaning more and more people got into purity culture. Which brings us nicely on to the Middle Ages – the era where slutshaming gets *really* heavy.

Roman shame, meet purity culture

It's during the Middle Ages or medieval period (roughly 500–1500) that slutshaming starts to look a whole lot like it does today. In fact, it's scary how little has changed in around a thousand years. The Middle Ages is defined as the period between the ancient and modern world, and Janega says this era basically took everything Rome did and 'slapped a bunch of Christianity on top'.

Throughout the Middle Ages, slutshaming continued to be a powerful way of keeping women in what the men, the philosophers and the religious leaders believed to be a woman's place. And where was that? Under the watchful eye of a man, who could make sure they weren't getting up to no good. What was 'no good', you ask? Sex.

With the shift to Christianity, the focus became making sure women were abiding to purity culture. They needed to reinforce the idea that women weren't allowed to have sex before marriage, and so they scared them into submission with threats of eternal damnation. To really drive this home, both men *and* women were scolded for sexual activity before marriage.

This ultimately led people to believe that the best men – the most noble and pure in society – were the ones who didn't have sex at all: those who joined the clergy and married God. Priests, basically. They were the only good guys. Men who got married were second best. And anyone else having any more sex than that was a slut.

'They believed sluts were fully carnal, just giving in to their sinful nature and the sensuality of the world around them,' Janega adds.

In the medieval period, it was also believed that sex was almost like a gateway to further sinning, such as gluttony (greed) and sloth (laziness), and that anyone possessing these traits would be a hindrance to society.

Both sexes were controlled by these regulations and strong 'values'. But, as always, women were more vilified when they didn't meet society's standards. Any woman who enjoyed sex in a way that wasn't God-approved was considered a sex worker, a threat to men and, ultimately, worthless.

Perhaps the strangest part of all this slutshaming is that in the medieval years people *loved* sex. They consistently bent their own rules so that they could have lots of sneaky sex, all the while proclaiming sex to be sin. In fact, it was particularly common for rich men and women, especially noblemen, to find ways to be a slut and get the sexual pleasure they so desperately wanted on the down-low.

Poetry, roses and sex parties

Much like Frances Carr's first marriage, a lot of 'marriages' between the richest people in medieval society looked more like a business transaction or political agreement than an actual relationship based on love. This left a lot of rich people in marriages that didn't give them joy, both in general life and in the bedroom.

And what's a posh medieval woman to do if she's not getting the sexual pleasure she wants?

Have you heard the phrase 'courtly love' before? It might conjure up images of rose petals in beautiful manors, with couples pursuing each other romantically. And you'd be half right to think of this.

The true history of sluts

Because marriages among rich people, especially royalty, tended to lack real love, courtly love (parties where people were encouraged to express admiration for one another) became spaces where married women could finally experience real romance.

They were also, however, basically medieval sex parties, and that's the part that gets missed from the history books.

Janega explains that courtly love pretty much hinged on unmarried men hooking up with married women. A bunch of them all around the same age would meet up in a noble household and court one another, often exchanging romantic poetry and roses before having sex.

Rich folk in medieval times had found themselves a nice loophole. (This seems to happen a lot once people realize they would actually quite like to have the sex they've been denying themselves.) Because sex *within* marriage was all about procreation, these horny medieval women figured that other types of sex would be allowed outside it, especially sex that wasn't penetrative (penis-inside-vagina).

Christianity put penetration on a pedestal as the true, pure, ultimate sex and determined that everything else wasn't 'real' sex. So no harm done, if married women receive oral sex at a party from a nice unmarried man, right?

The people who engaged in courtly love felt they were doing nothing wrong. Their role in society and dedication to religion couldn't come into question, as far as they were concerned. They were still upholding their duties at home and looking after their husbands and kids, and having procreative sex with their husbands. They were simply seeking the romance they were missing elsewhere. It was basically the medieval form of swinging, but without consent from the husbands.

The poetry and other pieces exchanged within these parties soon became a literary genre and the men who wrote them became known as the courtly love poets. Their work was eventually passed down to the middle classes, almost like their equivalent of *Fifty Shades of Grey*.

Where the word 'slut' comes in

At some point, we did stop branding all women who have sex as sex workers and started calling them other words, like sluts, slags, hoes, nymphos or even skets (as mentioned earlier, this is an English working-class term). This was by no means progression, but it certainly was *something*.

It was none other than William Shakespeare who brought the word 'slut' as we understand it today into the world in the sixteenth century. Before then, the word 'slut' had a very different meaning, referring to a woman who was dirty, untidy or lazy.

The true history of sluts

The phrase 'slut's pennies' describes the hard knots in bread from a housewife's poor kneading, and 'slut's wool' is dust that hadn't been cleaned from the floor. So, essentially, if you weren't good at making food and didn't have a clean house, you were a slut. It looks like I'm a slut in every definition of the word. This association of sluts with untidiness continued for many years, even until the eighteenth century, when Samuel Johnson's *A Dictionary of the English Language*, the first to be published (1755), defined a slut as a lazy housekeeper.

But Shakespeare provided the first recorded use of it to mean 'promiscuous woman'. Shakespeare was obviously a brilliant playwright during the sixteenth century, who brought us amazing plays like *Twelfth Night* and *Romeo and Juliet*, which were so good that they still influence our literature and media today. But he was also unfortunately a big old slutshamer, despite being a bit of a slut himself. It's clear from his works that he wasn't a fan of women who deviated from sexual norms or enjoyed sex outside of marriage (which is funny, because he writes about it a lot).

In his play *As You Like It*, he wrote, 'Well, praised be the gods for thy foulness; sluttishness may come hereafter. But be it as it may be, I will marry thee; and to that end I have been with Sir Oliver Martext, the vicar of the next village, who hath promis'd to meet me in this place of the forest, and to couple us.'

Shakespeare's works continued to feature slutshaming heavily. In fact, in *Much Ado About Nothing* a woman is egregiously slutshamed by her fiancé and father, based on an unreliable rumour about her sex life. The play's villain, Don John, tells Claudio that his fiancée, Hero, cheated on him and is no longer a virgin. Then Claudio freaks out and all hell breaks loose.

'Death is the fairest cover for her shame,' Hero's dad, Leonato, asserts in the play's fourth act.

While this play may be fictional, it's representative of how women were treated – and continue to be treated – for having 'out of the ordinary' sex lives.

The slutshaming of Anne Boleyn

Shakespeare's material involving sluts may explain some of the slutshaming that was going on in his time, the Tudor era. Anne Boleyn was Queen of England from 1533 to 1536. She was the second wife of King Henry VIII, and she was slutshamed so brutally that her treatment is still being discussed among historians today. In the book *The Jezebel Effect: Why the Slut Shaming of Famous Queens Still Matters*, anthropologist and biologist Kyra Cornelius Kramer notes how Anne Boleyn was ruthlessly slutshamed during this period in history.

The true history of sluts

Kramer writes that in 1532, during an Easter sermon, the priest, named William Peto, preached to his congregation, among whom Henry VIII and Anne Boleyn were sitting, that Henry VIII and Anne Boleyn 'were just like the Old Testament tyrant Ahab and his painted queen Jezebel'.

This was a pretty harsh statement, as, in the Bible, Ahab was presented as a wicked king who had turned away from God. It was clearly an insult to Henry and a jab at him for breaking away from Catholicism (he famously created the Church of England so he could divorce his first wife, Catherine of Aragon).

Kramer argues that Anne Boleyn came off worse in this statement, however. 'Jezebel [whom Anne was compared to] was considered worse because she was seen as the harlot who had used sex to enslave Ahab and turn him from the Lord,' writes Kramer. 'Anne, like Jezebel, was therefore the scheming temptress who had dragged a formerly good king down into the muck with her womanly wiles.'

Though there's buckets of historical evidence to say Anne Boleyn did no such thing, her reputation as a jezebel and a harlot (basically, a slut) clung to her name until her death, and for centuries thereafter.

Even celebrated historians are guilty of slutshaming Anne Boleyn. She is, in the opinion of many, 'the most controversial woman in

English history', purely because of her alleged sexual behaviour and the accusations of adultery, for which there is no basis.

Kramer says that Anne has been labelled 'a whore, a home wrecker, a soulless schemer, a horrible person who stole someone's husband', despite clear evidence that Anne did not actually do the things she was accused of doing.

Eventually, Anne Boleyn was executed on the order of none other than her husband, Henry VIII, who cited adultery as the reason for her public beheading. These accusations were based on rumour and many historians believe it was Henry's own wandering eye that ultimately led to Anne's death. He had already caught the attention of his next wife, so he needed to get rid of Boleyn somehow. So we have yet another historical man-slut hypocritically pointing the finger at a woman's sluttiness.

Burn the sluts

By the sixteenth century, slutshaming had become even more intense, as America's purity culture hard-launched and women across the world were forced to undergo virginity tests for the first time (see Chapter Two). This was especially prevalent in New England, where having sex before marriage was considered the ultimate sin.

Young adults in America fought back against virginity tests with 'junketing', which was where groups of girls and boys gathered to laugh, dance and tell sex jokes. And it was the dancing part that really got the authorities worked up. In Salem, Massachusetts, a Puritan preacher (a member of a religious group of English Protestants in the late sixteenth and seventeenth centuries who had high moral beliefs, especially about self-indulgence and sex) called Increase Mather really kicked off about it and told his many followers that dancing was basically the gateway drug to sex and would get you a one-way ticket to hell. He was a bit melodramatic.

It was then that witch trials began rippling through America and Europe, including the UK. Witch trials were a misogynistic practice in which people would target women who didn't fit into society and accuse them of witchcraft. Women who danced, women who had sex, women who lived independently and happily without a husband: they were considered witches.

One of the worst cases of witch trials was the Salem witch trials in America, as it became known, which was a series of hearings and prosecutions of people accused of witchcraft in colonial Massachusetts between February 1692 and May 1693. More than 200 people were accused. Thirty people were found guilty, nineteen of whom were executed by hanging. It was the deadliest witch trial in the history of colonial North America.

These women would be judged by a jury made up entirely of men. And the punishments for being considered a witch – which often relied on the testimony of eyewitnesses who had seen their supposed 'acts of witchcraft' – ranged from being publicly whipped, branded or even sentenced to death, via burning or drowning.

In *Witches, Sluts, Feminists: Conjuring the Sex Positive*, Kristen J. Sollée notes that the majority of so-called witches who were rounded up on both sides of the Atlantic were sluts. These societies believed that women who had babies, raised children, managed domestic chores and remained subservient to their husbands were good Christian housewives. Any woman brave enough to venture outside these norms would have been considered a slut and could have been accused of witchcraft. Men outed women as witches back then because they found them to be a threat to the status quo (the patriarchy). Slutshaming (or framing) them was the easiest way to take them down.

Even today, a beautiful and seductive woman is often described as 'bewitching' or 'enchanting' – words that imply a woman's sexuality is inherently wicked, linked to some kind of trickery.

On International Women's Day in March 2022, the then First Minister of Scotland, Nicola Sturgeon, issued an apology to the 4,000 people in the country, the vast majority being women, who were convicted and often executed under the Scottish Witchcraft Act of 1563.

'Those who met this fate were not witches, they were people, and they were overwhelmingly women,' Nicola Sturgeon said in the

Guardian. 'At a time when women were not even allowed to speak as witnesses in a courtroom, they were accused and killed because they were poor, different, vulnerable, or in many cases just because they were women.'

According to the Free Speech Center at Middle Tennessee State University, many judges, juries and accusers had publicly apologized in Salem, too, towards the end of the seventeenth century, but they note the apologies were of little comfort to affected families. By 1711, the state had exonerated the accused from all wrongdoing and offered financial compensation to surviving family members. In 2002, the Massachusetts state legislature officially cleared the names of the last of the accused witches.

Sluts are unhygienic

At the turn of the twentieth century, slutshaming began to influence the medical world, and slutty women were blamed for a vast uptick in the spreading of STIs in the UK and the USA.

This really began in Victorian London. A weird old time, the Crimean War of 1854–56 was in action between Russia and an alliance of the Ottoman Empire (Turkey), France, the UK and Sardinia-Piedmont (Northern Italy), and the troops were coming home with not only bucketloads of war trauma but also bouts of STIs, namely syphilis and gonorrhea.

If it's not treated, syphilis can cause serious and potentially life-threatening problems. And one in five soldiers had it. With such high transmission numbers and high stakes, it's no wonder Parliament wanted it gone. So in 1864, they created the Contagious Diseases Act to protect people from infection. The act meant that women suspected of prostitution were expected to register with the police and submit to an invasive medical examination. The legislation also meant police officers could arrest any woman suspected of being a common sex worker, regardless of whether they actually had a disease. Once arrested, the women would have to endure a medical examination and if they were found to be infected, they would be confined in a locked hospital until they recovered – sometimes for as long as a year.

Men, on the other hand, were never arrested or detained for soliciting those sex workers, nor for having an STI. All the blame was shifted on to women, especially working-class women and sex workers.

By the turn of the twentieth century, this idea of sluts being unhygienic and dangerous to a man's well-being was still being upheld across the globe. In 1937, the American sex hygiene film *Damaged Goods,* in which the lead character has an affair and contracts syphilis, became one of the most watched of its kind. This film was created to teach American enlisted soldiers about the effects of venereal disease (VD) and the types of women who might carry them. Those women were sex workers and, by extension, the poor.

In *Damaged Goods*, a middle-class soldier contracts an STI from a working-class sex worker who describes herself as 'too poor to get cured', so she lives with her disease and says she'll 'jump off a bridge' when she is caught. Ultimately, the messaging of the film was that she ruined the posh guy's marriage, and life, through the spread of the infection.

The research paper 'Deconstructing the "Low Other" in the First Wave of Sex Hygiene Films (1914–1919)' notes films like these, especially *Damaged Goods*, made classism worse in America, with people viewing the working class as 'nests for disease'.

'Just because she's a nice girl doesn't mean you can't get venereal disease,' a VD educational poster of the period boldly claimed. The running theme through exploitation films and posters such as these was that female sexuality is dirty and a serious threat to men.

And this brings us to the present day. Slutshaming has unfortunately not changed all that much over thousands of years. Women still fall victim to sexual rumour and public shaming about their sex lives, as happened to Anne Boleyn. Women are still conflated with sex workers – who also deserve respect – for enjoying sex with people they don't share a connection with. And many of the problematic assumptions around class we've explored still exist today (see Chapter Six).

But understanding this history puts us in a good position. There is power in knowing where these harmful ideas come from. And we can use this power to protect ourselves, to stand up for others, to call people out, and to fight slutshaming once and for all.

Slutshaming around the world

We can see the impact of purity culture and our deep history of slutshaming women when we examine the language used today for sexually expressive women all across the world. Age-old discrimination against sex workers (known as whorephobia) and the poor, and ideas about women being 'used up' if they have sex, are still evident in modern word choices.

Let's take a look at the specific words and phrases we use for sluts around the world. Some are terms that imply that sexually expressive women are dirty, others suggest they are animals. Some mystify them, like the word 'witch', while others completely dehumanize them.

Dirty

- slut, 'promiscuous woman', in English (coming from the fourteenth-century word for 'poor woman' or 'untidy woman')
- *sürtük*, 'vagrant, dirty', in Turkish
- *szmata*, 'slut', in Polish (literally translates to 'cloth' or 'rag'; also used to describe an easy win)
- *schlampe*, 'messy woman', in German
- شرموطه (sharmut), 'slut', in Arabic (meaning 'cloth' or 'rag')
- 公共厕所 (gōnggòng cèsuǒ), 'public toilet', in Mandarin

Sex workers

- whore, 'prostitute', in English (now used for sex workers and promiscuous women alike)
- 'Whore' is used across the world but has varying etymologies:
- قحبة (qaḥba), 'whore' (comes from the word for coughing in Moroccan Arabic. Believed to relate to the practice of sex workers discreetly coughing to signal potential customers)
- *puta*, 'slut', in Spanish (ironically comes from the Latin word for 'pure', as well as in Italian (*putana*) and Arabic (عاهرة/āhira). In French, 'pure' (*putain*) was used for 'prostitute' too, but this is now a general curse word, similar to 'fuck'
- *malaya*, 'prostitute', in Swahili (coming from the word for 'independent')
- *glädjeflicka*, 'prostitute', in Swedish (comes from the word for 'joyful girl')

Animals

- *porca*, 'pig', in Italian
- *troia*, a pig cooked with chicken inside it, in Italian (this offensive phrase comes from the Trojan horse myth, where pigs were seen as dirty, especially when stuffed with other animals)
- *piranha*, the flesh-eating fish, in Brazilian Portuguese
- *panopuu*, 'fucking tree', in Finnish
- 野鸡 (yě jī), 'wild chicken', in Cantonese
- *zorra*, 'female fox', in Spanish
- τσούλα (tsoúla), 'goat', in Greek

Objects

- village bike, in English, used to suggest 'everyone has had a ride' on a woman. This idea is also used in Finland, Slovakia and Spain (*la bici del pueblo*)
- *stadens madrass*, 'town mattress', in Swedish
- *Dorfmatratze*, 'village mattress', in German
- *jakorasia*, 'shared box', in Finnish
- *catin*, 'vessel', in French
- *kiberenge*, 'trolley care', in Swahili

Based on sex/genitals

- fanny like a hippo's yawn, in English
- basement slut, in English (specifically for women who like anal – most used in the USA)
- 'having sex with her would be like throwing a hot dog down a corridor' in English, also used in Italy (*fare sesso con te sarebbe come lanciare un salame in un corridoio*, changing 'hot dog' for 'salami') and Germany (*vagina, als würde man in einer Turnhalle eine Wurst werfen*, changing 'corridor' for 'gym')
- *avoir le vagin qui baille* ('to have a yawning vagina'), in French
- *suelta*, 'loose', in Chilean Spanish

Moving around

- *passeggiatrice*, 'woman who passes through', in Italian
- *pobehlica*, 'run-around woman', in Slovakian
- *flyfille*, 'a fly', in Norwegian (comes from *fille*, which refers to a used rag)

Magical

- trollop, in English (coming from Icelandic and Germanic language, meaning 'troll who enchants')
- *pūtanā*, in Hindi (lit. 'putrefaction' is a rakshasi, or demoness, who was killed after trying to kill the infant-god Krishna by breastfeeding him poisoned milk)
- *sirena*, 'siren', in Italian (a mythological creature similar to a mermaid who tricks men into drowning through seduction)

Others

- sket, short for skettel, a woman who wears dancehall clothes, in English (comes from the Caribbean and is commonly used in English in the UK)
- *ligger runt*, 'lays around', in Swedish
- *garota de programa*, 'programme girl', in Portuguese
- جنده (jende), 'overused', in Farsi
- خراب #(ḵarāb), 'broken', in Farsi
- זונה (zonah), 'foodmonger' in Hebrew

- *una come hombres*, literally means 'man eater', in Mexican Spanish
- *iödva püksikummida*, someone with loose-fitting pants, in Estonian
- *yollu*, 'has already come a long way', in Turkish
- *chomino*, 'slut', in Castilian and Andaluz Spanish (coming from sailors travelling past ports and shouting 'Show me now!' at the women, asking them to flash their genitals)
- *dziwka*, 'slut', in Polish (comes from the word for 'girl')

So much of this language is influenced by purity culture, loaded with assumptions about loose vaginas, and using terms like 'used', 'damaged' and 'dirty', and conflating women's sexuality with magic. Purity culture is right there in the language we use every day.

None of this is to say that you shouldn't use slang words. Of course, slang isn't inherently bad. Slang turns up in our language for all sorts of positive reasons. It's used to form communities and to communicate safely within those communities too. In fact, back in the 1960s, those working in the sex industry – along with queer people – developed their own slang for certain words, almost creating their own secret language. Called 'Polari', the language was a purposely confusing mixture of English slang, cockney rhyming slang, Romani and Yiddish. Speaking in this tongue meant that people could speak freely to other sex workers without persecution.

However, you can make better, more informed choices about which slang words and phrases you use if you know what they mean and where they come from. This can help us judge when certain words are appropriate, or inappropriate, to use.

4.

Sluts online

It's early 2020, and my mum and I are making sausage sandwiches on the grill. We live almost 200 miles apart, so when I visit, we like to do normal family things around the house rather than big, expensive, fancy activities. Making breakfast and having a cup of coffee in the mornings while we both scroll through social media is one of them. It makes it feel as though I still live with her.

But this breakfast was rudely interrupted. I received a message from a man on Instagram who was asking me for writing advice. When I accepted his message request, though, he quickly followed up with a video of him masturbating. It was extremely graphic, close-ups and all. I'd received unsolicited nudes – both images and videos – from men on the internet before, but this was the most detailed and most frightening video.

I tried to stand up for myself. I told him that not one but two women had now been forced to see his penis without consenting, and that what he'd done was horrific. His response: 'I thought you would have liked it, slut.'

I've been sharing my writing, and my personal life, on the internet for ten years. There have always been people who have sexually harassed me in response, but this increased significantly when my content pivoted to reporting sex and relationships, and when my follower count started to go up on X (formerly Twitter) and Instagram.

From the very first vibrator recommendation I shared on Instagram, or issue in the sex industry I investigated for a popular digital publication, I've been called a slut by strangers online.

If the history of slutshaming has taught us anything, it's that we have been condemning female sexuality and shaming anyone who doesn't appear to fit sexual norms since long before the smartphone showed up. But the arrival of social media has significantly changed how slutshaming happens, how it's received, and even how we speak about it.

Someone calls a woman a 'slut' or 'whore' on X (formerly Twitter) almost 10,000 times per day.

According to a 2016 study, *200,000* aggressive tweets were sent using those specific insults in a given month. If you're counting, that's about seven abusive tweets per minute, or about 9,500 a day. What's worse is that half of the offenders were women.

Seventy-two per cent of women across the UK, the European Union, the USA, Australia and New Zealand report receiving unsolicited nudes online like I did, a phenomenon commonly dubbed 'cyber flashing'. Often people cyber-flash others simply to hurt them, laud power over them or humiliate them. And in my case, to slutshame me.

The internet has become a breeding ground for slutshaming due to its anonymity and rapid dissemination of content, and to amplify the real-life experiences that happen offline. In fact, one group of researchers, in the paper 'Shame transfigured: Slut-shaming from Rome to cyberspace', describes it as a digital manifestation of the slutshaming of the Roman Empire.

The internet is still a fairly new place, and while it has advanced our communication and access to information in so many positive ways, it's important to understand how we could be using it to unintentionally replicate and heighten the bad parts of the real world, particularly when it comes to slutshaming. Then we can work to stop it.

Send nudes?

It can be exciting to send nude pictures of yourself to a partner or upload a suggestive photograph on social media. We've all had moments when we've got new lingerie or have taken a great beach pic on holiday and we're really feeling ourselves. Choosing outfits, angles and poses that bring out our best features can help us to see the beauty in our bodies. When it's taken for a partner, there's a glorious mixture of dopamine, sexual charging and empowerment when you and someone you love, or are interested in, are flirting and exchanging sexy images. It's teasing and titillating, like a digital precursor to eventual in-person intimacy, akin to selecting the perfect lingerie set and outfit before a romantic date.

For some couples, especially long-distance couples, nude-exchanging is even the centre of their sex lives. In the modern day, creating and sharing nudes is as much a sexual act as having oral sex.

But nude-sharing comes with a lot of danger. If you're under eighteen, taking photos of yourself naked is illegal in the UK, the USA, Australia, New Zealand, most of mainland Europe and in Japan. In the UK and the USA specifically, it's considered the production of child pornography. So you can be arrested for taking nudes if you're not an adult.

Further dangers come from sharing these nudes. You can't always trust partners, no matter how much you love them, and they love you, to keep those images to themselves. According to RMIT University, one in ten Australian women have had a nude image they sent to a partner shared with other people without their consent, along with one in twenty-five American women, according to a study published by the Data & Society Research Institute. And in the UK, one in seven women have experienced the same thing, says research from domestic violence charity Refuge. This specific act of violence is usually referred to as 'revenge porn'.

Revenge porn is defined legally as 'the act of sharing intimate pictures or videos of someone either on or offline without their consent, to cause embarrassment and distress'.

Forty-six states in the USA have laws against revenge porn. And the UK, Japan, Australia and New Zealand have criminalized this too. Surprisingly, at the time of writing mainland Europe does not have any firm laws against it, but this is likely to change soon. Several forms of cyberviolence like revenge porn and online harassment could become criminal offences, as the majority of lawmakers in EU committees have drafted the first-ever EU law to protect women from these acts.

Ninety per cent of women and seventy-five per cent of men in the UK and the USA have chosen to send nudes to someone, along with five in ten women under thirty in Australia. Yet, despite how common it is for both men and women, when women choose to send nudes they are often slutshamed for it.

When I was at school, it seemed that nearly every week there was a new case of a girl whose nudes had been sent around the whole school. To this day, I still think of these girls – especially the one who didn't come to college for a while after a video she'd shared in confidence with a boy she was dating was circulated among thousands of students. Almost ten years after the incident, she got married and had a baby; my friend's response was, 'I wonder if her husband's seen that video.'

One study, 'Slut Shaming in Adolescence: A Violence against Girls and Its Impact on Their Health', says the internet has offered teenagers new ways to slutshame each other. Boys who want to bully girls who have shared intimate photos with them can do it all too easily with the click of a button. And the trauma can last a lifetime. The research shows that teenage girls can become victims of unwanted dissemination, coercion and blackmail as a result of sexting and nude-swapping, while teenage boys are unlikely to suffer the same backlash. 'While it normalises it for boys, girls become victims of slutshaming,' it concludes.

Slutshaming has become part and parcel of adolescent cyber bullying. In fact, many girls will likely be sexualized on the internet, including being called a slut – or a slag, hoe, whore or other synonyms – by the time they're just twelve years old.

The study 'Why did she send it in the first place? Victim blame in the context of "revenge porn" ', found that people generally lacked sympathy for victims of non-consensual nude-sharing, specifically because they were naked. They also found that participants tended to assume the victim was promiscuous and were to blame for the image being shared.

It's common for girls who've sent nudes, or had nudes non-consensually spread around, to hear slutshaming phrases like:

- 'What did you expect?'
- 'You shouldn't have sent nudes in the first place.'
- 'She was asking for it.'

We saw this when a website entirely centred around revenge porn was created in 2010 by internet personality Hunter Moore named Is Anyone Up? The website featured stolen and hacked nude images and videos of women, mostly taken by vengeful ex-boyfriends, and Moore actively encouraged submissions to continue, eventually raking in 200 submissions of stolen nudes per day.

When asked why he created the site, Moore said, 'It all started with me hating some dumb bitch who broke my heart,' as shown in the documentary *The Most Hated Man On the Internet* (2022), which explores the website's, and Moore's, eventual downfall. This quote speaks to how visceral rape culture really is and how easy it is to perpetuate it online without a second thought. Predators brazenly admit that they see acts of rape and sexual assault as a justifiable way to get revenge on women who dare to reject them, and that doing it online – hiding behind a profile while they attack from the safety of their own homes – makes them feel powerful.

Similar to the Is Anyone Up? scandal, in 2015 a phenomenon that came to be known as The Fappening took place, which saw hundreds of celebrities' phones being hacked and their nude photos published online.

In both cases, women have fought back valiantly. Is Anyone Up? was taken down via the extensive media campaign of one victim's mother, Charlotte Laws. Her daughter Kayla's phone was hacked, and her nudes were stolen and published on the site. Charlotte took it upon herself to start her own investigation, which was eventually handed over to the FBI and caught the attention of notorious hacker group Anonymous, who closed down Moore's internet servers. In 2014, Moore was charged for his crimes and sentenced to two and a half years in prison.

Sluts online

Actress Jennifer Lawrence, one of the victims of The Fappening, bravely spoke out against the slutshaming rhetoric she had experienced as a result. Speaking to *Vanity Fair*, she said, 'Just because I'm a public figure, just because I'm an actress, does not mean that I asked for this. It does not mean that it comes with the territory. It's my body, and it should be my choice, and the fact that it is not my choice is absolutely disgusting . . . It is not a scandal. It is a sex crime. It is a sexual violation. It's disgusting. The law needs to be changed, and we need to change.'

Eventually, in 2018, Ryan Collins, a thirty-six-year-old man from Pennsylvania, USA, was charged for the hacking.

But rape culture, and the slutshaming that keeps it afloat, didn't rise or die with Hunter Moore or The Fappening. It's still all around us, and it continues to persist and evolve within the digital world.

Jess Davies, a broadcaster, content creator and former glamour model, recently presented a BBC documentary investigating revenge porn after her own intimate images were shared non-consensually in online forums. Davies told me she had been e-whored, which is when nudes are stolen and sold to make money.

As part of the investigation, she spoke to a man who had illegally shared women's images online before. His response when questioned was, 'It's just cam girls, OnlyFans girls and girls who already post their body online.' In other words, because he did this to women who are sluts, he didn't see that sharing private images of them non-consensually was a problem.

Don't get me wrong – sending nudes isn't innately bad if you're an adult and it is safe to do so. Safe sexting and image-sharing can be an empowering and joyful way to extend your boundaries of intimacy and connect with someone. Yet, because of the world we live in, where slutshaming and punishing women for sexual expression is rife, there are dangers attached and it is important that we know these risks.

Nonetheless, if you are someone who has taken nude photos before, whether you've consensually sent them to a partner, to multiple people, or just taken them for yourself, you *never* deserve to be shamed for this.

Safe places

Slutshaming feels different on the internet compared with real life. Those who grew up in the earlier stages of social media's arrival, like me, will probably remember school assemblies where the weight of the internet and its permanent record were gravely shared with us. We watched as a teacher squeezed toothpaste out of a tube, letting it spill everywhere. The metaphor was clear: once you've emptied it, you can't put it back in.

Sluts online

I think that's what makes slutshaming comments on the internet, as well as other types of discrimination online, feel so uniquely painful and frightening. It's the idea that someone feels so passionately about denouncing your lifestyle that they're willing to risk their own public record as well as yours, permanently.

It's also incredibly intrusive. Many people, myself included, use social media as a safe place – somewhere to foster community and share content with like-minded people and have enlightening, open discussions. When someone invades that space with the intention of hurting you, it can feel like a stranger broke into your house and destroyed it.

However, research has shown that many people who slutshame on the internet aren't necessarily thinking about their actions at all. The internet has granted anyone with Wi-Fi access the ability to share their personal beliefs publicly, often on impulse, with little thought about the content or the impact this might have on others. This is, in part, due to something called the anonymity and online disinhibition effect.

Coined by psychologist John Suler in his 2004 paper 'The Online Disinhibition Effect', this is the idea that the internet allows users to remain relatively anonymous. It makes them feel less constrained by social norms, and so they may engage in behaviour they wouldn't in face-to-face interactions. He wrote that many people on the internet live by a 'you can't see me and you don't know me' ethos, making them feel free to say whatever the hell they like. This means slutshaming can take on even more vicious and upsetting forms online.

And when slutshaming happens online, it becomes more accessible and less avoidable. Basically, it's *louder*. Social media platforms like Facebook, Instagram, X (formerly Twitter) and Snapchat have become breeding grounds for slutshaming. Photos, videos or posts can be easily shared, commented on or mocked, making it difficult for victims to escape public scrutiny and humiliation. With the rapid and widespread nature of social media, the impact of slutshaming is exacerbated. It can feel like everyone is talking about you, and you're surrounded with nowhere to escape.

And while people who slutshame online can feel protected by their anonymous accounts, this doesn't apply to the victims. Sexually expressive women with prominent social media profiles often share personal details about their lives on those same platforms where shamers come to hurt them.

Actress Emily Atack talked about this on author and influencer Florence Given's podcast, *Exactly. With Florence Given*. She described how the horror of being slutshamed and abused online is often followed by the realization that this person could also work out personal details about you, like where you live. 'Yeah, I can block them, but what if this person comes to my house?' she says. The people being slutshamed aren't granted the same protection as the people trolling and slutshaming them anonymously. This adds a layer of danger and fear to the slutshaming experienced online.

Sexy jail

Thankfully, the internet is also the ideal place to combat slutshaming. Being online presents new opportunities for connection and information-sharing, and social media grants us access to people who have similar interests and goals. That means that we can curate an online world that reflects our own feelings and beliefs, find people who feel the same, and build a community who can rally together to fight slutshaming.

For example, the sex positive movement has found a home on the internet, particularly on Instagram and TikTok. What was once a taboo is now an open topic about which conversation is encouraged, all thanks to a small army of sex positive influencers, educators, advocates and workers. Their goal is to help people explore their sexuality and teach them everything they might want to know about sex that they didn't learn at school. The sex positive movement offers an inclusive community for celebrating sex, free of shame.

There are various people leading the charge in this space. There's Sex Positive Families, who give parents the tools to avoid sex negative behaviour – including slutshaming – and ensure they don't pass those messages on to their kids. There's an influencer duo called Come Curious who create sex positive content on Instagram and host a podcast, *F**ks Given*, where they discuss the best, worst and first experiences of sex with a range of guests, unapologetically sharing the good, bad and ugly. And there are influencers such as Ruby Rare, an accredited sex educator who creates accessible, fun content about sex on her Instagram. Then there's Oloni, an influencer who has created an online space where women can share their funniest, wildest and most heartwarming sex stories with a like-minded community. Sex positive accounts combine safety with sexiness, and create judgement-free zones where people can learn and share information about sex.

One of the key accounts contributing to the anti-slutshaming conversation is Slut Social. The team behind Slut Social has reclaimed the word 'slut' like many feminists before it, flipping its history on its head by taking it back as an empowering term to describe people who enjoy and celebrate shame-free sex. Slut Social share memes that poke fun at people who slutshame and celebrate all facets of sex for the joys it can bring. They also host regular in-person workshops in London and offer sex workshops (Skool 4 Sluts), which they describe as 'slutty sex education'.

Accounts like these have allowed many women to educate themselves and reclaim their sexuality after growing up with slutshaming all around them.

Unfortunately, however, many of these sex positive groups and individuals find their content being censored by social media companies. Dr Carolina Are, a criminologist specializing in online censorship, tells me that social media algorithms automatically punish sexual behaviour.

'Social media has helped some people embrace the concept of being a slut, and even reclaim the term,' Are says. 'But social media companies and their algorithmic biases ruin that.'

According to *WIRED*, Meta reportedly automatically bans content that's identified as sexual by AI technology. Dr Are says the result of this is that sex positive social media accounts are being removed from these platforms. In June 2023, Meta started deleting sex positive accounts from Instagram without warning. And while this has happened in the past, this was one of the largest mass account pullings so far.

Accounts are still disappearing, and in 2021 Are's account was deleted, which she believes was due to her content being mistaken for sexual solicitation. Now her account is restricted because of flagged 'nudity and sexual activity'. But while Are supports sex workers, she herself has no experience of it. Rather, her Instagram is mostly videos of her pole-dancing routines, lessons where she offers pole-dancing tutorials to her followers, and content about her academic research in criminology. Writing on Instagram about the restrictions on her account, she says, 'Well, I'm in sexy jail!'

Many of the other users affected by this were also not soliciting sex at all. They were sharing art, education, lingerie recommendations or working with sex toy brands.

Mitch Henderson, a Meta spokesperson, told *WIRED*, 'We understand our platforms play an important role in helping people express themselves and connect with communities. While we allow sex positive content and discussion, we have rules in place around nudity and sexual solicitation to ensure content is appropriate for everyone, particularly young people. A number of the accounts brought to our attention were removed in error and have been reinstated.'

OK, great, so they reinstated the accounts that *weren't* involved in sexual solicitation. But what about the ones that were? Sexual solicitation is merely sex work, and includes users like OnlyFans models, camgirls (girls who pose and perform for webcams) and escorts. The actual laws around sexual solicitation vary from country to country. In the USA, it is mostly illegal, as is also the case in certain countries in mainland Europe, such as Ukraine and Iceland. While in Holland, Germany and the UK (excluding Northern Ireland) it is legal. Yet Meta was removing the accounts of people from those countries where sex solicitation *is* allowed by law. In other words, Meta is making their own rules up by punishing sex work in countries where it is legal. Technically, they can do this as a private company, but it leaves the sex workers with nowhere else to go.

TikTok also doesn't allow sex content to thrive on its platform, even if it's educational. Instead, sex positive communities are forced underground.

Similarly, Google News – the news filter for the world's most popular online search engine – say in their publishing guidelines that sexually explicit content is considered 'inappropriate'. It has suggested that many news publications may have their articles hidden from Google searches, blocking off search traffic to their websites if they include sexually explicit content, which they have not defined. This has created a culture of fear regarding any content to do with sex, no matter how positive or important it is to share. This censorship is unfortunately worsened by bills enacted to protect women. The UK's Online Safety Act was passed in 2024 and criminalizes cyberflashing (sending unsolicited nude photos), but means all sexual content online is targeted and deemed unsafe, regardless of the actual content. Ironically, it's a digital slutshamer.

But we're still putting the information out there regardless. Sex workers, educators, creators, artists and writers like me try to get around these blockades by disguising their content. In videos sharing sexcapade stories, TikTok users will typically use the word 'seggs' rather than 'sex', with the 'seggs' tag having 2.9 billion views at the time of writing, and 'seggseducation' having 2.2 billion. Editors of news outlets and magazines have shared with me the ways they sneak past Google's restrictions, disguising sex content as other types of content (like technology or culture) and by writing less sexually explicit headlines.

It's inspiring to see so many creators continuing to put out the sex information that people want and deserve in the face of scrutiny and censorship, and it's something I've proudly been a part of in educational articles and social media posts I've written.

However, having to create content that tricks algorithms into letting you keep your platform at all speaks to the anti-sex culture online. And it's very dangerous. Censoring key words like 'sex' means sex education online is less discoverable. Those who aren't 'in the know' about the code words will be unable to find it. It's like a digital version of the whisper networks and secret slang used by sex workers and the LGBTQ+ community in the 1970s and 1980s.

People deserve access to online information about sex, especially when, as recently as 2023, governing bodies across the UK, Europe and the USA have restricted sex education in schools in very harmful ways (see Chapter Seven).

We have to take a stand against this censorship. Exercising your sexual freedom by just being you is a protest. If we're clear in our position that everyone deserves access to and knowledge about sex, we can win this fight.

Stars, sex tape scandals and society's double standards

Influencers and media personalities play a significant role in shaping public opinion on everything from fashion and politics to attitudes towards sex and sexuality. Singer songwriter Ariana Grande has used her platform to challenge slutshaming after being repeatedly shamed by journalists who have questioned her number of partners or her clothing choices. In an Instagram post, she wrote, 'If a woman has a lot of sex (or any sex for that matter), she's a slut. If a man has sex, he's a STUD, a BOSSSSSS, a KING.'

In 2016, Grande also took to Facebook to share an anti-slutshaming message. 'When will people stop being offended by women showing skin/expressing sexuality? Men take their shirts off/express their sexuality on stage, in videos, on Instagram, anywhere they want to . . . all. the. time.' She continued, 'The double standard is so boring and exhausting. With all due respect, I think it's time you get your head out of your ass. ♡ woman [sic] can love their bodies too!! ♡'

Unfortunately, some celebrities use their platforms to slutshame others. Leaked sex tapes have long plagued celebrity culture. They are lauded as just another piece of hot gossip, while celebrities – mostly women – suffer the consequences of being exposed without their consent.

From the '90s through to the mid 2000s, there was an influx of sex tapes being leaked and posted online completely shamelessly. And the celebrities involved were *always* slutshamed. Sorry, let me correct myself. The female celebrities involved were slutshamed. The men were, of course, celebrated.

The clearest example of this is in the case of model and actress Pamela Anderson and musician Tommy Lee. In 1995, a sex tape of Anderson and Lee from their honeymoon was leaked after a disgruntled contractor broke into their house and stole it. Anderson struggled to be taken seriously in her acting career after the sex tape was leaked. She even lost out on roles as a direct result of it. In a now-deleted post, musician Courtney Love described the impact the video had on Pamela, saying, 'It destroyed my friend Pamela's life. Utterly.'

It's been over twenty years since the tape was first seen by the world, but Anderson cannot avoid slutshaming comments about it to this day. In 2016, she wrote an op-ed calling for the pornography industry to be reformed after her partner had struggled with a porn fixation. Anderson isn't a sexuality expert, so I will admit the op-ed had some holes where scientific evidence should have been. Yet there are plenty of clumsy celebrity op-eds out there that don't trigger the same level of backlash that Anderson received. Her intelligence was insulted, and her sex tape history was ridiculed and, ultimately, used as a reason not to trust her opinions.

Sluts online

In contrast, Lee reportedly revelled in the fame he received from the tape. And when Disney+ created a TV programme about the event, he said, 'Let everyone know we did it first. Before the Kardashians, before anyone else. Let the mother-f***ers know, we broke the internet first,' according to a source in the *Mirror*.

Another clear example of this was the leaking in 2004 of American media personality Paris Hilton's sex tape with professional poker player Rick Salomon, who released the tape himself. In an interview with *Vanity Fair* in April 2021, Paris described having post-traumatic stress disorder from the video, saying, 'It was a private experience between two people [. . .] You love someone, you trust someone and to have your trust betrayed like that and for the whole world to be watching and laughing. It was even more hurtful to me to have these people think that I did this on purpose – that killed me.'

Yet, like Lee, Salomon gained money and fame (and zero slutshaming) as a result of the tape. He even released and sold a longer version of the tape titled *1 Night in Paris*.

In an article about the slutshaming surrounding celebrity sex tapes, *Glamour UK* journalist Lucy Morgan reports that the video of Paris and Rick was later recognized at the Adult Video News Awards, winning three awards, including Best Overall Marketing Campaign – Individual Project. Yes, you read that correctly.

The sex tape won an award, even though it was widely known that Hilton had not consented to the film being shared.

Morgan also writes that American media personality Kim Kardashian, another victim of a leaked celebrity sex tape in 2007, is still slutshamed for the video now, some sixteen years later.

Since the tape was leaked online, Kardashian has mothered four children, started the process to become a lawyer, used her platform to create change in the criminal justice system in America, and launched multiple successful skincare, beauty and shapewear brands. She also produces and stars in one of the most successful reality TV series of all time. Yet, in 2023, her sex tape was dominating the headlines once again.

In an interview with *Vanity Fair*, her ex-husband and rapper, Kanye West, talked about how much the sex tape still hurt Kim during their marriage. The fallout from this interview was anything but sympathetic. People responded with speculation that Kardashian had secretly leaked the video herself to get attention and money, and they commented on her lack of intelligence. They suggested she had to use her body instead of her brains to succeed, and refused her any empathy over this completely violating experience.

Kim Kardashian is continually branded a slut and little else. In 2016, a ten-foot-high mural of her was painted on a wall in

Melbourne and was defaced with the word SLUT in block capitals less than twenty-four hours after it was put up.

Kardashian used her platform to speak out on the matter. Later that week, she posted an essay on her blog to say she wouldn't let her 'life be dictated' by slutshamers. 'I am empowered by my sexuality,' she wrote. 'I am empowered by feeling comfortable in my skin. I am empowered by showing the world my flaws and not being afraid of what anyone is going to say about me. And I hope that through this platform I have been given, I can encourage the same empowerment for girls and women all over the world.'

Yet in the public's eyes, women like Pamela Anderson, Paris Hilton and Kim Kardashian, who have had their sexuality displayed publicly without their permission, don't get to share their opinions. Not about sex, nor about their own experiences of the sex tapes, nor anything else. They don't get to be intelligent or interesting. They don't get to receive praise for their accomplishments. They are only ever sluts.

The underlying theme across all these stories is the same. Being a slut is wrong, and if you use the internet to sexually express yourself by sharing nudes or suggestive imagery, whatever happens next is your fault.

This is wrong.

No one ever deserves to be slutshamed for their sexual expression, on or offline. No one ever deserves to be shamed for finding and enjoying their sexual selves. And no one should ever be subjected to non-consensual sharing of nudes.

It's time we make slutshaming itself a shameful act, rather than sexual expression – online as well as in real life. We must call out people who perpetuate rape culture on the internet, correct our friends who lack sympathy for victims of online abuse and slutshaming, and call our friends into sex positive spaces online.

'Broken bitches'

To understand how slutshaming has evolved online over the last few years, we have to talk about Andrew Tate.

If you're lucky enough to not know who Andrew Tate is, he's a British-American businessman who used to be a professional kickboxer. Now, he's one of the biggest social media personalities in the world, renowned for his videos on how to be an alpha male, how men can find 'high value women' and for speaking proudly about being a misogynist. At the time of writing, Tate has recently been charged with rape, human trafficking and forming an organized crime group to sexually exploit women. He is currently on house arrest awaiting a trial for those crimes and has denied all allegations.

Despite this, he has over 8.5 million followers on X (formerly Twitter) alone, plus more on other social media platforms. He's also in the top five most googled people in the USA and is confirmed to be the number one most influential person in the USA at the time of writing. In fact, according to statistics provided by YouGov in 2023, a quarter of men in the UK aged between eighteen and twenty-nine who had heard of Tate agreed with his views on how women should be treated. And twenty-eight per cent of men between thirty and thirty-nine supported his views too. What views are they, you ask?

Here are just a few things he's said about sluts:

- 'I would not see male infidelity as even one per cent as disgusting as female infidelity because female infidelity involves emotion.'
- 'Any woman who can say, "I fuck dudes and I don't care about it" is fundamentally broken. Her soul is broken. I don't want no broken bitch near me.'
- 'In the modern world if I meet a girl who's thirty-three and single, I know the amount of dick that's been through her before me is just simply unattractive.'

He also has a lot of interesting (read: absolutely disgusting) ideas about why sluts don't deserve sympathy if they are raped:

- 'Women have been exchanging sex for opportunity for a very long time. Some [rape victims] did this. [They] weren't abused.'
- 'Of course now [rape victims] will say they were abused. However at the time it was a simple exchange they partook in voluntarily. Not all. But some.'
- 'If you put yourself in a position to be raped, you must bare [sic] some responsibility.'
- 'No woman should be abused regardless. However with sexual assault they want to put zero blame on the victim whatsoever.'
- 'If I left a million dollars outside my front door, when it got stolen people would say: "Why was it there? Irresponsible." '

The slutshaming is confidently littered throughout his posts and interviews. And his main goals are to 'make men alpha again' (did they ever stop being so?) and to 'reinstate women as the second sex' (again, did that ever go away?).

To me, Tate shouldn't be anywhere near as influential as he is because his entire output revolves around trying to make patriarchy happen when it's literally already in place. I'd laugh at him if he wasn't so scary.

Yet, as the stats show, his influence is huge. But why? On Vox's podcast *Today, Explained*, Robert Lawson, an associate professor in sociolinguistics and author of *Language and Mediated: Cultures,*

Contexts, Constraints Masculinities, said Andrew Tate is so appealing to his internet-based audience because of a concept called 'aggrieved entitlement'. This is the belief that over the course of the last few decades the world has changed in a way that has decentred white men and moved them to the margins of society.

Someone like Tate is 'attractive to men' because he plays on this myth that women have 'taken over', and he promises to put men back on top. He basically tells them, 'You're important, you're needed, and your masculinity is needed to fight against the changes that are happening in the world. The world is no longer for you but you can change that.'

Tate is a dangerous person with a massive reach, and he seems to have a lot of men – and some women too – in the palm of his hand. When we look at how conversations about sex on apps like TikTok are changing, we can see his influence, and the influence of others like him, taking shape in very harmful ways.

One example of this is a recent obsession on TikTok with body counts. On the *Full Send Podcast*, Tate said, 'A body count is probably the number one most easiest way to judge the value of a female ... I think ninety-nine per cent of the world's problems would be solved if females walked through life with their body count on their forehead because it would prevent disintegration of morals ... All the idiocy would disappear, all the degeneracy would disappear, families would return.'

I'm not sure why Tate thinks that sitting across the table from your nan with the number of men you've slept with written on your head would help bring the family together. Sounds like it would just make for quite an awkward Christmas dinner . . .

Unfortunately, his beliefs are spreading across TikTok. At the time of writing, TikToks with the 'body count' hashtag have been viewed 6 million times around the world in the past week. And in the last three years videos with this hashtag have been viewed 917 million times. In many of these videos, men take to the streets to ask other men what their ideal body count would be for a woman and discuss the answers accordingly.

I have said it once and I will say it again. No matter what anyone on any social media platform tells you, these are the facts:

- The number of people you have slept with doesn't determine your value. You are not a product; you don't have a 'value'
- The number of people you have slept with does not impact your ability to be a good partner
- Men who judge you for the number of people you have slept with, or don't want to connect with you because of it, do not deserve you

Sex sells, but so does slutshaming

Even among the lifestyle influencers who post about lighter things, slutshaming is a big part of their content. Recently, I was doom-scrolling through Facebook when I found myself on the video section. In one clip, a blonde woman was sharing her and her husband's experiences with infertility to show the 'real, difficult side' of trying to conceive.

At first, the video seemed like a genuinely helpful insight into the pressure that comes with trying to have a baby. That was, until she shared what 'worked for her' in terms of 'turning her infertility around'. She claimed that her inability to get pregnant was a punishment for her promiscuity in her early twenties. She advised her followers that giving up 'one-night stands' and avoiding 'having sex before there's commitment' is the best way for women to protect their future fertility. She said this to her 200,000 followers.

Many women hold serious fears over their fertility. A small-scale study showed that almost half of sixteen- to twenty-four-year-olds were worried about their future ability to conceive, even if they had no real reason to believe they could be infertile. A likely cause of this is that girls and women are regularly reminded of the 'biological clock' (the idea that women have less chance of conceiving naturally the older they get). These influencers prey on this vulnerability to get away with slutshaming.

And some influencers knowingly trick women with misinformation because they can make a lot of money from it. Among the most well-known purity influencers is a pair of Texas sisters running the Girl Defined social media platforms. They peddle messages encouraging both modesty and shame in sex and relationships with men.

Bethany Beal and Kristen Clark, the sisters behind Girl Defined, focus most of their content on heteronormative relationships, in which they use purity culture myths to encourage their largely female audience to control their sexual urges and remain abstinent until marriage. Their posts are littered with homophobia and transphobia, and they seem to purposely reinforce harmful gender stereotypes, including the idea that women shouldn't be sexually expressive, but men sure can be. They have some 159,000 YouTube subscribers consuming their content.

Since their arrival on the internet, more purity influencers have popped up all over TikTok, some with a similar reach to Girl Defined, some smaller. Type 'protecting your energy' into TikTok and you'll soon find myriad videos of people pushing purity culture myths around body counts and soul ties, while pretending they're promoting sex positive feminism.

But, thankfully, there are plenty of influencers also using the internet to dispel those myths and even celebrate being a slut.

Slut era

In a more positive turn of events, in 2022 the online world saw the concept of sluttiness turned on its head and reframed as a form of self-love and acceptance.

And I am here for it.

In spite of the dark parts of the internet plagued by Tate and those sneaky slutshaming influencers, it seems that masses of young people are working hard to spread messages of sex positivity.

At the beginning of summer, actor Dylan O'Brien tweeted the phrase 'slut era', which seemed to be the start of this welcome shift. It was the signal to strip down, show off your best slutty outfits and start having as much great sex as you'd like. 'Slut era' soon became the mantra for those ready to maximize pleasure during the summer, and the trend is showing no signs of stopping.

Gradually, the slut-era trend transformed into something of a light-hearted joke. Many women on the internet poked fun at the internal desire to be a carefree pleasure-seeking slut, but not having the energy or resources to make it happen. Tweets like, ' "slut era," I say as I delete his number, put fluffy socks on and crawl into bed' garnered hundreds of thousands of retweets.

This is something Ruby Rare has talked about too in her 'Sexy Sermon' on the joy of being a 'part time slut' and a 'slut on sabbatical'.

Whichever side of the trend you're on – fluffy socks or casual sex – the many users getting involved have reframed the definition of slut to mean 'someone who does whatever the hell they want, and unapologetically seeks pleasure'. During a time of Andrew Tate, a renewed interest in purity culture and body count obsessions, this is nothing short of revolutionary and gives me a tremendous amount of hope for a shame-free future.

Where do we go from here?

It's clear the internet is a double-edged sword, simultaneously perpetuating the problem of slutshaming while being a fundamental tool in fighting against it.

While the internet and social media have allowed for the rapid spread of negative content, they have also enabled awareness and education, and provided a home for supportive communities. Though slutshaming online might feel loud sometimes, here are some ways we can drown out the noise:

- Follow sex positive accounts
- Start your own sex positive account
- Call out slutshaming behaviour online and report any users who are spreading harmful or dangerous beliefs
- Call your friends in to learn more
- Join communities that are fighting slutshaming and see what you can do to help

- Campaign for online safety by sharing everything you've learned about slutshaming and how to fight it on your own platforms

To combat online slutshaming effectively, a collective effort is required, and we all need to work together. Every person should have access to sex positive content that challenges slutshaming and aims to create a safer, more respectful and empathetic world.

Our digital lives are part of our sex lives now. For some of us, our digital experiences are key parts of learning about sex and discovering who we are. We all deserve to explore that safely.

5.

Boys will be boys, but girls will be sluts

There are times where I've been on the receiving end of a slutshaming comment, often when I'm with a group of male friends, and it's had a different feeling to it. It's been more bitter, more insidious, like a secret meaning is at play. While the comment might sound like disapproval of my sex life, with a 'You've shagged *how many* people?', or disappointment in my clothing choices, with a 'Put some clothes on,' I know it's not actually about that.

Because, often, there are men around me doing the exact same thing. They're talking about the multiple women they've slept with recently, and they tumbled out of the house wearing whatever was clean. They're, quite frankly, acting like sluts. They're flirting in the bar, openly talking about what they'd like to do sexually to the women they're interested in. We're *all* flirting and talking about sex. But I'm the one being belittled for it.

I didn't know this when I was a teenager. I just thought I was a bad person. But now I know that these specific, visceral moments of slutshaming are not really about sex at all. They are about gender.

Gender-based discrimination is where women are stereotyped, belittled and treated differently because of their gender. And when a man slutshames a woman, sexism is usually what's truly at play. As we'll come to explore, there are rules written into the very fabric of our society that allow certain sexual behaviour for men, and don't allow it for women, leaving girls and women as key targets of slutshaming.

If you're a girl or woman reading this, you may have also had moments where, like me, you've been made to feel like you're doing 'too much' because of your sex life, what you're wearing or the ways you've spoken about dating in public too. The reason this is affecting so many of us is because slutshaming is more about gender than it is about sex. To interrogate why that is and fight back, we need to look at the ways misogyny and sex shame overlap.

Boys will be boys, but girls will be sluts

Now, you might be a man reading this and thinking, 'Well, I've been slutshamed!' or you might know a man who has experienced it. When men are slutshamed, though, it's usually down to the personal opinion of the shamer. That's not to say slutshaming a man is acceptable – it never is – but we do need to recognize that the slutshaming of men is not systemic (i.e. deeply embedded into society's systems, such as healthcare or education). Instead, it is usually coming from someone's individual judgement and values.

Slutshaming women, on the other hand, is woven into the tapestry of society. And it's time we changed that.

Mind the gap

Did you know that women earn less than men in every country in the entire world?

The pay gaps range all the way from a 1.17 per cent difference in Belgium to thirty-one per cent in South Korea. From a global perspective, on average, women earn seventy-seven cents for every dollar earned by men. At the current rate, it is estimated that it will take 257 years to close the global gender pay gap.

You might be wondering how this all relates to slutshaming. Well, when we slutshame, we are upholding the patriarchy. Because the patriarchy is responsible for all of these gender inequalities, such as pay gaps, there's a domino effect at play.

When we slutshame women, we're not only vilifying them for their sex lives but contributing to all these other injustices too, limiting their financial freedom, their access to healthcare, their job opportunities and so much more.

When we slutshame, we basically help the patriarchy to persist.

Don't play in the mud

From an incredibly early age, we are given a specific set of rules for boys and a different set of rules for girls, known as gender roles. Gender roles are sets of rules that tell us how we're expected to act, speak, dress, groom and conduct ourselves based on our assigned sex at birth. For example, girls and women were (and still are) generally expected to dress in typically feminine attire (such as dresses and skirts) and embody qualities like politeness, tidiness, a nurturing spirit and a strong desire to raise a family. All while not complaining about the fact that they're doing the washing-up for the hundredth time.

Boys and men, on the other hand, were (and, again, still are) encouraged to be boisterous and display attributes such as strength, power and competitiveness. They are also discouraged from openly displaying emotion and affection, especially towards other men.

Boys will be boys, but girls will be sluts

And these expectations translate to rules about sexual expression too. Michael Yates, a clinical psychologist specializing in sexual issues from The Havelock Clinic, tells me that we first learn about the gender-based rules for sexual expression when we play as children. Yes, really.

Remember when you were a kid, and playing in the mud, rolling around and getting filthy with your friends, felt amazing? Do you remember when you first realized you weren't supposed to be doing it any more?

Yates explains that even as young children we're aware of what's deemed OK for boys and what's 'not for girls'. At a certain age, during childhood, most girls are discouraged from getting dirty and messy, and from other activities that aren't seen as 'ladylike'. Boys, on the other hand, are allowed to be loud and dirty, and be kids.

Girls are expected to grow up very quickly and be small, quiet, clean and take up as little space as possible by not raising their voice or drawing attention to themselves, so they don't seem over-confident or brash. And who gets to use that space instead? Boys and men.

As children, we are constantly reminded of these gender roles through various cues. For example, when girls tell adults they've been bullied, hurt or offended by a boy, a common response is for them to be told something like 'boys will be boys', an infamous phrase used to normalize cruel behaviour from boys and encourage girls not to make a fuss.

Toys marketed to boys also tend to involve action, aggression and excitement, from monster trucks and wrestler action figures to toy racing cars. Girl toys, on the other hand, are often pink and passive, emphasizing beauty and fashion, and encouraging young girls to develop their nurturing side, from dress-up dolls to baby dolls that girls are supposed to 'look after' for fun.

This might seem insignificant – I can hear the cries of 'They're just children's toys!' already – but it's through constant cues like this that we learn where society believes a woman's place is, and where a man's is.

So how does this translate to sex? Well, gender roles, especially under the watchful eye of purity culture, result in a pretty serious and unrelenting pleasure gap, which is a worldwide phenomenon.

Society is hinged on what men need from us – nurture, sensitivity, passivity – and this leads to a hyperfocus on men's sexual needs too. Which, in heterosexual sex, means a focus on penetration. This negatively impacts pleasure for women. The vast majority (eighty-one per cent) of women cannot orgasm through penetration alone and need clitoral stimulation. But under these gender norms, these acts of pleasure get sidelined (it's all about the penis, remember?!) and regarded as 'foreplay', a predecessor to sex rather than 'actual sex'.

And this has contributed to a pleasure gap between men and women: in the UK, men are almost twice as likely to have an orgasm during sex with a woman than a woman is when having sex with a man. Interestingly, queer people are less likely to prioritize penis-in-vagina penetration, and they experience the most pleasure of all, especially women who have sex with women, who statistically have more orgasms than anyone else. Lesbians are truly winning.

In the Netherlands and Belgium, condom company Durex found that twenty-eight per cent of men said they were unable to orgasm, compared to seventy-five per cent of women.

And the research paper 'Sexual Behavior in the USA: Results from a National Probability Sample of Men and Women Ages 14–94' shows that in the USA, cis women are four times more likely than cis men to find sex unenjoyable.

In addition, a 2020 survey from the Japan Family Planning Association found that, in Japan, men have concerns about how long they will last during sex. In contrast, women's concerns were mostly related to pleasure, such as 'not being able to feel pleasure' and 'not being able to reach orgasm'.

The pleasure gap is everywhere, but the sexual double standards unfortunately don't stop there. We also learn from the patriarchy that casual sex is OK for men, but not women, which we find out at a young age when we hear that abundance in general is OK for men, but not women.

If men are allowed to express themselves – to be loud, to be dirty, to overconsume (be it food or video games) – it's no surprise they take this into the bedroom too. Yates explains that sex is how adults play, so we take the rules we learned in the playground into our adult lives. We soon learn that men can be loud about the sex they have, and greedy in how much they have it. Their messiness is fine. Women's messiness – which includes casual sex – is not.

Broken locks and master keys

Have you ever heard the phrase 'a lock that can be opened by any key is a broken lock, but a key that can open any door is a masterkey'? I know I have. This phrase is everywhere. It's on viral TikToks. Reddit. All over student forums, where teenagers go to seek sex advice. And it's one of the clearest examples of sexual double standards for men and women.

If you're unfamiliar with the phrase, it essentially compares locks with vaginas and keys with penises. Charming, isn't it?

Boys will be boys, but girls will be sluts

A penis is a 'masterkey' if it's able to unlock any door (vagina). But any woman who possesses a lock (vagina) so easily jimmied open is a useless, broken lock. It's truly grim to compare any person – man or woman – to an inanimate object in this way. And that's before we confront the use of words like 'broken' and 'master'. Women are endlessly subjected to language like this when they have sex with a lot of men. Meanwhile, men are typically celebrated for such behaviour – they are masters, kings, absolute lads.

A recent study published in the *Journal of Sex Research* illustrates this sexual double standard. It found that men and women in the UK both frequently lie about the number of sexual partners they've had. But while women usually lie by pretending the number is lower than it really is, men do the opposite. They pretend to have had more sexual partners than they really have.

It was discovered that both lied because of societal expectations. Women know that a higher social value is achieved by having slept with fewer people, and men know the opposite to be true for them.

This idea is reinforced in dating too. In a study from Cornell University into how people view sluts, participants were asked to choose the ideal partner from three women: one was 'promiscuous' (meaning she had a lot of current sexual partners), another was 'promiscuous but reformed' (meaning she used to have sex with a lot of partners but she now doesn't) and the third was 'not promiscuous at all' (meaning she doesn't have a lot of sexual partners and never has).

The women's profiles were also populated with details about hobbies and goals, making them all vibrant and interesting. Only six per cent of men considered the promiscuous woman as a long-term partner, while eighty per cent of men considered the 'never promiscuous' woman as their ideal.

In another study from the University of Texas at El Paso, women were equally judgemental of men who were promiscuous, but interestingly much more interested in the 'reformed promiscuous' person. Thirty-two per cent of women didn't mind dating a man who'd had over forty partners, as long as he was looking to settle down now. But only fourteen per cent of men would consider dating a woman in the same boat.

Slutshaming and dating

This idea that it's innately bad to be a slut can affect our dating lives. Twenty-six-year-old Jodie* tells me she recently went on a blind date and one of the first questions he asked her was what her body count was – before he even asked anything about her job. She ended up answering because she was just completely stunned. He replied, 'It's higher than I'd usually like, but I can deal with it.' Unsurprisingly, there was no second date.

Boys will be boys, but girls will be sluts

Body count discourse is just one strand of double standards in sex and dating, with unfair and conflicting rules for men and women. Other double standards include men being able to take their shirts off in public without getting arrested, being able to ask for what they want in the bedroom without judgement and, in some cases, even demanding it.

These double standards around body counts rely on the (completely false) idea that men have naturally higher sex drives than women.

In reality, no one has a 'low' or 'high' libido of any kind – something that has been explained by Dr Karen Gurney, known as the Sex Doctor, in her book, *Mind the Gap: The Truth about Desire and How to Futureproof Your Sex Life*. The idea of libido or 'sex drive' is not actually scientifically backed. Instead of drive, what we actually have is desire. Sex is not needed to survive like food or water, therefore we don't have unstoppable urges (no matter what some people might tell you).

The desire to have sex exists on a moving spectrum, rather than a 'low' or 'high' basis. One singular person is unlikely to have a high sex drive their entire life. Instead, it moves up and down constantly. For men *and* for women.

Yet, because the myth that men have naturally high sex drives and women don't is so persistent, we allow men to be sluts. We wave it off with phrases like 'boys will be boys' and 'Men just can't help themselves, can they?' But they can. Men have sex with lots of people for the same reason women do: because they want to. Because it's fun.

Meanwhile, women who have sex with lots of people are, you guessed it: sluts.

We see this double standard all the time in the media. Take Taylor Swift, for instance. She has been consistently scrutinized by other celebrities, the media and the public for having several high-profile relationships over her almost-ten-year career.

And the slutshaming towards Taylor has been nothing short of ruthless. In June 2013, American retail company Abercrombie & Fitch sold shirts saying 'more boyfriends than t.s.' And the Westboro Baptist Church leader Ben Phelps called Swift the 'poster child for the young whores of doomed America', before announcing plans to protest at her concert.

In her 2016 *Vogue* interview for their series '73 Questions', the singer was asked what she'd tell her nineteen-year-old self. Swift replied, 'Hey, you're going to date just like a normal twenty-something should be allowed to, but you're going to be a national lightning rod for slutshaming.'

Boys will be boys, but girls will be sluts

Somehow Taylor's eleven studio albums and multiple Guinness World Records, including the highest-grossing music tour ever, are eclipsed by her dating life.

In a 2019 interview with Zane Lowe on Apple Music's *Beats 1* show, she said she was forever being slutshamed for a dating life that was 'completely normal except for the fact it routinely made headlines'. She also pointed out that slutshaming is a common way to 'take a woman who's doing her job and succeeding and completely minimize that skill'.

She added that she believes 'everyone in their darkest moments loves to slutshame women' and that it isn't just her; it happens to many young female artists.

The double standard is crystal clear when we look at *Saturday Night Live* comedian Pete Davidson, who has had just as many high-profile relationships as Taylor Swift, if not more. Yet he is praised for his behaviour. Davidson is called 'iconic' and a 'king' on social media for 'being able' to 'pull' the likes of Emily Ratajkowski, Ariana Grande and Kim Kardashian.

Davidson has only ever shared one side effect of dating a lot of people in the public eye – that potential partners expect him to be an amazing boyfriend who is incredible in bed, and he's not always sure that he matches up to his reputation.

Having such public interest in your romantic relationships will undeniably put pressure on you, whether you're a man or a woman. But while Swift's career has been overshadowed at times and her reputation has been smeared by this scrutiny, Davidson's experience is starkly different.

Now, don't get me wrong. I am all for praising Davidson for his dating history. And honestly, I get why people are looking at him twice, now he's dated a few (incredible) celebrity women. People with a higher number of past relationships can be more confident when talking about their needs and can also bring more to the table (read: bedroom). Experience is very sexy to a lot of people, myself included, but the same celebration and allure of sexual abundance doesn't apply to women. And that's the problem.

'I'm not like other girls'

It is important to mention that it's not only men who slutshame women. You may have heard slutshaming referred to as a 'girl on girl' crime before, and that's because many women report being slutshamed by other women.

The aforementioned study from Cornell University found that most women view other women who have a lot of sexual partners as less trustworthy, bad partners and bad friends. Women who've had more than twenty sexual partners were even described as 'less competent and emotionally stable, less warm and more dominant' than women who'd had two sexual partners or less.

Slutshaming coming from women might seem odd to you. But from a young age, women are taught to see each other as competition – it's something that upholds the patriarchy. I mean, if we're too busy competing against one another, we'll never be able to take down the system that's holding us back!

Have you ever said or heard the phrase 'I'm not like other girls' before? I'm pretty sure I embarrassingly reblogged it on Tumblr back in the day.

So what does it mean when someone says this? Well, it implies that 'mainstream' women enjoy those stereotypically girly things, like shopping, the colour pink, make-up, you know the drill, but the person saying the phrase takes pride in not fitting that stereotype. So much so that they believe they are better than anyone who does.

One of the stereotypes included in this idea is that other women are 'too much drama' and that men make much better friends. This is often a way for women to seem like the 'cool girl' who has no problem hanging out with men, but it's at other women's expense. It says, 'Look at me, not her. She'll bring you drama like all women do, but I won't. I'm special.' This is misogynistic, as it perpetuates a few harmful stereotypes: that women can't be genuine friends, only competition, and that women bring men drama.

We can look at Taylor Swift again to see how this 'other girl' idea is so intertwined with slutshaming. Many female celebrities have attacked Swift in this specific 'I'm not like other girls' way. At the 70th Golden Globe Awards in 2013, host and comedian Tina Fey delivered a joke about Taylor following recent tabloid news claiming she had just broken up with Connor Kennedy. Fey warned that, given Swift's 'interest in guys', actor Michael J. Fox's son, who was escorting the award winners off the stage that evening, should stay away from her.

Fey was obviously kidding, and of course, as part of her job, she makes digs about lots of people. But when girls and women do what Fey did to another woman, pointing the finger at sexually expressive women critically, this is a way of distancing themselves and letting the world know they aren't like *that*. They are separating themselves from the slut.

Fey is a smart, vocal, talented and outspoken feminist, but rather than helping a woman who has been shamed for her sexuality, she reinforced the message – Taylor is a slut.

This happens because we've been raised in a patriarchal society that needs women to see each other as sexual competition. But female solidarity is a beautiful, powerful thing. To have women who wholly understand and support you is unparalleled. Why throw that away?

Why are we still here?

You may be wondering why gender roles and double standards are still a problem we face. We've had multiple waves of the feminist movement. You'd like to think that if you asked most people you passed on the street whether men and women are equal, they would say yes.

And many researchers question this too. We aren't hunter-gatherers any more. There's less fear about paternity certainty. Women work in the same industries as men. And people are exploring alternative relationship styles such as polyamory. So why are these double standards still knocking about?

Well, the 2012 study 'Biosocial Construction of Sex Differences and Similarities in Behaviour' argues that gender roles are now cultural, rather than biological or evolutionary, as they once were. What these researchers mean is that gender roles now exist to serve purity culture and patriarchy, rather than being products of evolution.

So, there's no real, helpful reason for gender roles to exist. And they hurt everyone involved. While women police themselves and each other, and feel compelled to hide any sexual expression to retain their value in society, men feel the same pressure in the opposite way. Men are forced to collect sexual experiences like Pokémon in order to increase their social value. Under these circumstances, no one is having the fun, joyful, carefree sex we all deserve.

In a patriarchal system, no one wins.

Killing the kraken

Now that we understand slutshaming's past and present, and the double standards that play a part, we can work on fighting against it. There are a number of actions you can take in your personal life, particularly among your friends, family and the people you're dating, to challenge harmful ideas, enjoy your own dating and sex life more, and even to make the world a better, more shame-free place.

Sex educator Erica Smith describes slutshaming as the tentacles of the 'monster that is purity culture'. And I find thinking of it as a giant, ugly, slimy kraken to be pretty accurate.

So, how can we slay this mythical beast?

- Call in your friends and share your knowledge about purity culture and slutshaming. Arm them with this knowledge too
- If you're comfortable and safe to do so, call people out when they say harmful things that perpetuate purity culture, gender roles, sexual myths and slutshaming values

Boys will be boys, but girls will be sluts

- Challenge your own thinking about your sex life or other people's. Does having a certain number of ex-partners really matter? Does it change who you (or they) are as a person, or are you simply growing and gaining experiences?
- When you hear people slutshame women but praise men for the same behaviour, point out the double standard
- Stop forcing the children in your lives into boxes. Let girls play in the same way that boys do. Listen to girls when they say boys have offended or upset them. Boys will not simply be boys
- Join the sex positive movement so you can be with like-minded people who understand that everyone should be able to sexually express themselves, regardless of gender

Sex is a part of who we are, and gender roles should not be allowed to eliminate that. We should never be made to feel as though we need to hide or cut off that part of ourselves to make others more comfortable.

6.

Slutshaming across the class divide

To say social class makes slutshaming complicated would be an understatement. 'Social class' refers to people within a society who are grouped by socioeconomic status (money, wealth and privilege). These classes can look very different depending on where in the world you live, and sociologists have lots of different ideas about how many class groups there are in each country and who fits into which bracket.

In the UK, for instance, some sociologists and philosophers believe there are only two social classes (the lower class and the higher class, or the bourgeoisie and the proletariat), while others believe there are five, or even seven. The most commonly used system in the UK splits everyone into four main classes:

- The lower class (a not very nice name for the long-term unemployed and homeless)
- The working class (unskilled or semi-skilled workers like labourers. You may hear them and the lower class both referred to as 'chavs')
- The middle class (working professionals like teachers and nurses – this is where most of Britain sits)
- The upper class (people with highly professional and sought-after jobs like barristers, or those from old money. You may hear them referred to as 'toffs') as well as aristocrats, who are connected to the Royal Family in some way

The USA and Japan also have the same four class groups, while in Australia there are different classes – the established affluent, emergent affluent, mobile middle, established middle and established working classes.

In general, those who are middle to upper class have more privileges in society than those in the working- and lower-class brackets. For example, those in higher social class groups are more likely to own a home, be able to afford childcare, go on holidays and save money.

Is capitalism ruining my sex life?

To understand how slutshaming intertwines with class systems, we first need to look at two very complicated beasts: capitalism and socialism.

Capitalism is a system that revolves around increasing state growth. By definition, in capitalism, important resources are owned by wealthy businesses and individuals rather than the public, which creates a hierarchy where poor people end up at the bottom of the food chain, with limited access to these resources. Capitalism is the creator of social class groups. Without capitalism, there's no hierarchy, and therefore no classism.

The opposite of capitalism is socialism. This is a different type of economic system in which property and resources are owned by the public or the state. Socialism is more about sharing a country's wealth evenly among people and ensuring all are treated fairly.

These are *very* simplified definitions, but we need to know the difference between these systems to understand how they have a huge influence on our day-to-day lives. It's these economic structures that determine our healthcare systems, judicial systems, education systems and more.

It's important that we discuss classism when investigating why slutshaming happens, because poor people, particularly poor women, are slutshamed uniquely. We have to consider them, along with anyone who isn't a cisgender, able-bodied, heterosexual, rich white man (and we will explore other minority groups and their experiences of slutshaming soon) to ensure that we're being considerate of absolutely everyone in our fight against shame.

Slutshaming is, after all, an intersectional issue. The term 'intersectionality' was coined by civil rights scholar Professor Kimberlé Crenshaw in 1989 and refers to the way different systems of discrimination can overlap and create extra layers of disadvantage for certain communities. For instance, if you are a working-class woman, you are likely to struggle with both sexism and classism. And if you are a working-class woman of colour, you are likely to struggle with sexism, classism and racism. If we want to confront and combat slutshaming head-on, we have to understand how it impacts marginalized people in different ways.

Feminist theologist Professor Elisabeth Schüssler Fiorenza coined the term 'kyriarchy' in 1992 to describe these multiple, interweaving systems of oppression – things like patriarchy, classism, racism, transphobia and colonialism (see Chapters Six to Eight), which all work together to oppress marginalized groups at once.

So, as well as the patriarchy, there are various systems working hard behind the scenes to keep slutshaming going. It's always important to consider those who might be suffering under oppressive systems that you are not and thinking about how you can help them too.

The vast majority of Western countries are under some form of capitalism, including the UK, the USA, Japan and most of the countries in the European Union. And the very foundations that capitalism is based on have warped our experiences of pleasure.

Breanne Fahs, Professor of Women and Gender Studies at Arizona State University, said in the *Boston Review* that the current era of capitalism (late-stage capitalism, which focuses on increasing consumerism), includes 'mind-numbing jobs, uneven shift work, punishingly long work hours, crazed connections to smartphones, soul-crushing commutes, low pay, and destructive coworker and customer interactions', so people generally hold less space in their lives for genuine social connection, including romantic and sexual relationships, or have deprioritized them.

She explains how capitalism categorizes sex with leisure and relaxation, which it demonizes as laziness.

While working in Japan to report on their sex culture, I was told by marketing consultants for sex toy brands in Asia – who would prefer to stay anonymous because of the difficulty of speaking out on subjects like this in Japan – that the country has an intense 'work hard, play hard' ethos.

Japanese salarymen (businessmen) who are in the upper class tend to work brutal hours, sometimes thirteen to fifteen hours per day, while their wives will typically stay at home, looking after the children. What they have found is that, typically, middle- to upper-class men in Japan have a much more active sex life than their wives. Unlike many countries in the West, sex toy purchasing (and using) is normalized among men in Japan, while it is shamed among women, and men regularly use sex work services to satisfy their desires.

Why? Well, this is where capitalism comes into play. One of the reasons women may have less colourful sex lives than men in Japan is because they don't have as intense a work culture as men do. 'The gruelling hours and expectations that come with work for Japanese men means the way they choose to play is justified. They can use toys, have lots of casual sex and have sex with sex workers. Meanwhile, women might be looked down on just for buying a sex toy or talking about sex because she's seen as a non-worker [and therefore not deserving],' one consultant said.

Capitalism and cross-country slutshaming

Because capitalism – and the gender roles that come with it – is making a real mess of sex, many sociologists and ethnographers believe that women would have better sex under socialism, where gender roles and class hierarchy, in theory, wouldn't exist.

Slutshaming across the class divide

We can start to see this in countries like Denmark, the UK, Hong Kong, Singapore, New Zealand, Australia, Switzerland, Canada and Ireland, which have a 'free market economy'. This is technically capitalism, but most of these countries adopt elements of socialism in certain areas. For example, many have state-owned services such as healthcare, transport, water and housing. Since the government controls a lot more in socialist societies, it can make better use of resources, thereby reducing the huge wealth gaps between the classes.

Kristen Ghodsee, author of *Why Women Have Better Sex Under Socialism*, explains that in free market countries like Iceland, Denmark and Holland, women have freer sex. While 'free sex' should be individually defined according to Ghodsee, in academic studies it refers to 'undiscriminating casual sex with any partner that they like'. Basically, it's slutty sex without the slutshaming – my personal utopia.

This is because when women have more economic freedom, they don't feel pressure to make sexual or romantic choices that will impact their financial and social status. Many women in capitalist countries have been found to make sexual decisions that increase their status or wealth. People from low socioeconomic backgrounds may have sex with richer or more socially 'valuable' partners in order to gain value or wealth themselves, whether it's by shagging their boss or joining in on the recent TikTok trend that saw young women travelling to the more affluent areas of their cities to update their dating app location settings and find richer matches.

Of course, as is the case with most academic studies, this is a generalization and by no means should it be taken as an assumption that all poor women are sluts who sleep with, date or marry rich men for financial gain. But class systems are complicated and generalizations help us to understand and talk about the experiences of different class groups more openly, which can ultimately help lead to equality.

Ghodsee notes how perceptions about women and their free sex lives can permeate across countries. She says that Denmark is a particularly interesting case study for slutshaming. Though women from Denmark are typically sexually freer than in other countries, people tend to associate this with being 'easy'. In other words, it's easy to get a Danish woman to agree to have sex with you. But that is not the case. She mentions that Roosh V, a male pick-up artist and blogger who writes books on how to have sex (or 'bang') multiple women in each country (he seems like a great guy), wrote that men shouldn't bother trying to have casual sex with women in Denmark, because his pick-up artist tricks didn't work there. He even specifically says in the book, 'the state takes care of women in Denmark, so they don't need us men'.

And Scandinavian and Eastern European women are often slutshamed in the way they are represented in the media. Early noughties kids grew up with *The Inbetweeners* (2008–10), a show about teenage boys trying to have sex for the first time. In one of the episodes, the main character, Jay, assumes he'll be able to have sex with Dutch women easily because they're 'properly filthy'. Similarly, in *Skins*, a show that ran from 2007 to 2013, about teenagers in Bristol navigating their lives, including sex, drugs, relationships, issues with school and mental health, the only Polish teenager in the show – who is unnamed – is portrayed as completely desperate to have sex with English boys. The only English words she understands are sexual words, and she strips naked at a house party, attempting to sleep with anyone she can.

Twenty-one-year-old Kasha, a student at Central Saint Martins in London, tells me she's experienced 'a lot of xenophobic slutshaming' ever since she moved to the UK from Poland. She soon noticed in her sixth form that people had preconceived ideas about Polish women and their sex lives, assuming she would be 'hardcore in bed' and that she had probably lost her virginity at age twelve. She said she was often the victim of cruel sexual rumours and comments.

How social class impacts your sex life

I grew up living in a council flat (a house built and owned by the British government). Whenever I've had sex, I can honestly say I've never thought about this flat, or the jobs my family worked, how much money they had, or what school I went to. I'm usually focusing on orgasming, I won't lie. But our social class, and all those parts of our lives that our class influences, actually has a *lot* to do with how we have sex, how we talk about it and who we choose to do it with.

The research paper 'Prevalence and correlates of "sexual competence" at first heterosexual intercourse among young people in Britain' has found that people from lower socioeconomic backgrounds tend to have sex for the first time at an earlier age than those from middle- or upper-class backgrounds, for example. This is, partly, because they typically mature earlier.

Dr Hannah Charnock, a lecturer in British History at the University of Bristol who researches the historical context behind sexual behaviours, adds that working-class or poor parents will generally have much less control over their children's dating lives when they grow up; rich parents are more likely to give their children criteria that their romantic partners must meet.

It has also been found that working-class parents are more likely to have sex positive households, where they allow their children to explore, letting their children's partners stay the night, and being more open and forthcoming about sex education and sharing information. This might be why working class people are more likely to be sexually expressive and have multiple sexual partners.

Slutshaming across the class divide

This might also explain why so many of my university pals, namely the posh ones, were horrified, and even a little judgemental at times, when I'd immediately call my mum after a drunken one-night stand or when I needed dating advice. They couldn't believe I was able to do this without 'getting into trouble'.

Charnock tells me that in a lot of working-class communities, early sexual debut can be a marker of social status, whereas the opposite is true in a lot of middle-class bubbles. However, she notes that, of course, these are generalizations. There are always going to be middle-class and working-class people who don't fit these prescriptions. Though most of this research tells us that working-class people are more likely to be sex positive and non-judgemental, it looks different from the outside, and working-class women face a very particular, harmful type of slutshaming.

When slutshaming is actually classism

It goes without saying that these statistics don't mean that everyone from a working-class background is having sex one way and middle-class people are having sex another. None of this is to say that posh people are doomed to unexciting sex lives, or that working-class women are always free. In fact, we'll get to why that's certainly *not* the case shortly. Someone's social background, of course, doesn't speak for everything.

Sure, a lot of the statistics and research does show that working-class women are likely to be more sexually expressive than middle-class people, but, firstly, it would be wrong to assume that this is true of *all* people within these social groups. Also, the problems come when this is judged by wider society as a bad thing. What should be celebrated as a positive aspect of working-class culture – community-based sexual education, fewer restrictions on who you get to have sex with, less chance of being judged within your class for having free sex – have been flipped into 'dirty and promiscuous' stereotypes that harm working-class women.

Everyone is different, and both sex and class are incredibly nuanced. It's never OK for anyone to assume anything about your sex life and especially not because of your social class. But they do. And, as a result, class also impacts how we are slutshamed.

The research study 'The Impact of Class and Sexuality-based Stereotyping' says it's a common assumption and stereotype that women from low socioeconomic backgrounds sleep around. The researchers say that media representations of working-class women usually involve them being 'difficult and promiscuous'. They add, 'Even when she is characterized in a well-intentioned, sympathetic manner, she is still seen as having little control over her sexual desires.'

We see the slutshaming of working-class women in pop culture all the time. Netflix's *Sex Education* was a show that ran from 2019 to 2023 about two students who start their own sex ed clinic at school. One of the main characters is a working-class schoolgirl called Maeve Wiley. She is significantly poorer than her peers and lives in a caravan, struggling to make rent after being abandoned by her family. And she is routinely slutshamed. Every comment, rumour and aggression sent her way is loaded with undertones aimed at her social class and her sexual expression.

Take, for instance, the scene when we meet Maeve as she passes the popular crowd. 'What a slag, look at that greasy hair. Maybe she can't afford shampoo,' is one of the first things we hear about her from another character, Ruby. 'I heard she sucked off twelve guys in ten minutes for a dare. [. . .] She's basically a nympho,' another character, Eric, iterates.

Maeve's class is continually used against her as she's slutshamed throughout *Sex Education*'s very first episode. Though other richer girls become victims of slutshaming, including when Ruby's nudes are sent around the school, it is always for sexual behaviour they have actually participated in and the slutshaming eventually disappears. The rumours about Maeve, however, stick around for the duration of the show, and they are always untrue. They are simply assumed because of her clothes, her living situation and her family dynamic. Basically, because she is poor.

The same thing happens in one of the most popular TV shows in the world: *Friends*. Out of the six friends, Phoebe Buffay is the only working-class woman. So it's telling that there are several instances throughout the show's ten seasons when the other (middle-class, male) characters judge her for her so-called promiscuity.

Phoebe used to be homeless, and she's portrayed as the goofy one who doesn't always know quite how to fit in among her group of privileged friends. She often slips up with social behaviour, and her sexual expression is seen as part of her 'weirdness'. Phoebe is the only female character to date multiple people at once and frequently experiment with casual sex. There are even episodes where her own friends call her a nympho and express concerns over her lack of long-term relationships. Yet they have no issue with Chandler's similar inexperience with long-term relationships – presumably because he's a middle-class man.

It's not a coincidence that the two poor women in these TV shows are the only ones to be routinely slutshamed. It is an accurate representation of the experiences of working-class women in real life.

A serious problem with this stereotype is that it can affect working-class women's sexual health and safety. The research paper 'Prevalence and correlates of "sexual competence" at first hetero-sexual intercourse among young people in Britain' found that many young working-class women have sex before reaching the legal age of consent, just like I did, and are less likely than middle-class people to have access to the resources, information or sex education to ask for what they want and protect themselves from unwanted pregnancy.

Working-class women are also, according to another research paper, 'Rape and Respectability: Ideas about Sexual Violence and Social Class', more likely to be sexually assaulted than middle- to upper-class people, which is a strong case for why more sex education, and conversations about class and its impact on sex, are so important.

Instead of fixating on harmful stereotypes based on people's social status, we should be having meaningful conversations about how we can *all* enjoy freedom and safety in our sex lives.

Dating across the class divide

Dating in heterosexual relationships is also rife with classism and slutshaming, especially when the man is from a higher socioeconomic background. Ghodsee explains that often the slutshaming can come from the families, when children disrupt their parents' expectations and date outside of their social class.

This affects both Phoebe Buffay and Maeve Wiley's characters. When Phoebe accidentally overshares about her sex life in front of her boyfriend's (extremely rich) parents in one episode of *Friends*, they cruelly tell him, 'You can have all the fun you like with that one' before suggesting they set him up with one of their rich friend's children once he's done with her.

And when Maeve begins a relationship with a popular, middle-class boy, he asks her to keep it a secret because they're from different worlds (presumably, he means social classes).

Ghodsee explains that this specific type of slutshaming is all about one thing: guarding wealth. Slutshaming working-class women, especially when it comes from families, is usually about hoarding wealth and keeping particular types of people from benefiting from their financial privilege.

Perhaps you're thinking that those with a lot of wealth have a right to guard their money. But it's classist and misogynistic to assume a working-class woman will use you for money and a rich person will not. It also perpetuates the offensive idea that 'there are women you can fuck and women you can marry', which is a well-known sexist idea that subjects poor women to mistreatment from men.

Middle-class parents typically, according to the study 'Social Class and Premarital Sexual Permissiveness: A Re-Examination', turn their nose up at interclass sexual relationships, sex before marriage, teenage sex and infidelity, much more than the working classes.

That might explain why forty-five per cent of upper-class participants in the research 'Opinions on relationships/marriages to different social classes in Great Britain 2017' said they would not be prepared to have a long-term relationship with someone from a different social class – and why Marie Bergström found in her book, *The New Laws of Love*, that dating app users often unconsciously filter out users from different social classes to their own.

All this means is that working-class people are slutshamed whenever they date outside of their class, and middle- to upper-class people are encouraged to choose status over love or attraction when it comes to finding a partner. In other words, nobody wins.

Council estates and single mothers

The 'poor slut' trope doesn't just exist on the screen. We often see this stereotype reinforced in the slutshaming of working-class mothers, especially single mothers, who are using the benefits system (referred to as 'welfare' in a lot of countries).

In 2008, British newspaper journalist Melanie Phillips suggested in the *Daily Mail* that women in council estates were not only sluts but that their promiscuity also made them unfit parents. She said that council estates are where 'generations of women have never known what it is to be loved and cherished by both their parents throughout their childhood' and that 'such women' cannot know how to parent their children. She added, 'These children are simply abandoned [. . .] as the transient men passing through their mothers' lives leave them with an ever-lengthening trail of "step-fathers" or "uncles".'

This showed the extreme lack of empathy people with class privilege sometimes have for lower-class women. Why is it a poor woman's fault if a man doesn't stick around after having children?

This idea of the sluttish, poor single mum is often seen onscreen as well. BBC's *Motherland* (2016–) is a show about a group of mothers (and one stay-at-home dad) who are 'in it together' as they navigate the difficulties of being a parent. There is one mum in the show who is obviously the odd one out, though: Liz. Unlike the other middle- to upper-class mums, who have huge suburban homes and either swanky jobs or husbands with swanky jobs, she is the only parent who is single, strapped for cash and living on cheap frozen food in her tiny flat. She also happens to be the only mum in the entire show – which to date spans three seasons – who gets slutshamed.

The other mothers presume she is a slut, staying as far away from her as possible, with one mother even spreading a false rumour that she has slept with one of the other mums' husbands. Liz explains it perfectly herself: 'I'm the only single mum so they're worried I'm gonna steal one of their fat husbands.'

As Owen Jones argues in *Chavs: The Demonization of the Working Class*, classism always seems to get a free pass when it comes to discriminating against others, and it often goes unchecked. By anyone. This is how TV shows get away with stereotypical characterizations, and it sets a precedent that it's OK to slutshame working-class women.

'She should be sterilised'

Recently, I've been joining a lot of Facebook groups. I'm not in my racist uncle era, don't worry. I've been looking for communities of people who are happily child-free so I can figure some difficult stuff out. My husband and I have long gone back and forth on whether or not we want to have kids and I thought joining groups representing both sides of the decision might offer me a clearer picture of what I want.

The group with the most members advertises itself as a 'judgement free, shame free community for child-free-by-choice people'. It mostly contains playful memes about what to say when a rude and out-of-touch family member interrogates you about when you're having kids. But it's also rife with slutshaming, classism and sometimes both at the same time.

In one post, a member photographed a woman selling crafts at a local market. In the photo, you can see a tip jar with a photo of a baby scan taped to it. A message in felt-tipped pen reads, 'Please consider tipping, 6 months pregnant.'

'She should be sterilised,' one comment reads in bold letters on the Facebook page. 'I suppose they expect us to raise their kids for them,' reads another one. I scroll further down. 'Why should I pay for her lifestyle when she can't close her legs?' another post reads.

You might assume these are lines from a dodgy bootleg of *The Handmaid's Tale*, but they're actually from a Facebook group made up of so-called feminists. Every post I just quoted was written by a woman.

As the woman is alone, they presume she is single. And as she's asking for money (politely, I might add), they presume she is poor. And the comments just get worse. 'I would take money out of the pot,' writes one user. 'Why doesn't she ask her five baby daddies for help,' another says.

A sneakily taken picture lacking any real context whatsoever has the power to draw up such vicious, classist slutshaming. I mean, how dare a poor woman have sex, right?

Similarly, a Facebook group titled 'Have you tried marrying the father?' has almost 50,000 global members and exists solely to slutshame single mothers. Posts include scrutinizing single mothers' dating app profiles and sharing women's social media posts wherein they complain about being mistreated by men (and blaming them for it).

It's clear what the thought cycle is here, which these people are trapped in. They assume the mothers will need financial assistance from the government, and they don't believe they should have to pay for these women's benefits via their taxes. But let's not get it twisted. People who make comments like this about working-class women are *not* concerned about their money being taken away. They simply don't believe that working-class women are equal to them. They believe they are superior to them.

The implication beneath these comments is clear: poor women don't deserve to be sexually expressive and they don't get to make mistakes in relationships the way rich people do. Why? Because they are poor.

Internalized slutshaming, meet internalized classism

Sociologist Ben Rogaly from the University of Sussex tells me that being class-shamed can have negative effects on a person's mental health and lead to them feeling isolated.

It makes sense. Classist slutshaming is why I've always felt awkward bringing up my single parentage on dates – I know that so many men assume that working-class women without fathers are promiscuous because of widespread classist ideas. Classist slutshaming is also why I've heard 'You can take the girl out of Telford . . .' (a common phrase used to poke fun at someone being

173

able to leave their home town but unable to escape its influence, usually aimed at people who live in 'shit hole' areas) so often when I've told what I thought was a fun sex anecdote to a friend.

Being slutshamed in this way burrows deep into our subconscious and affects our self-perception. It causes many working-class women to internalize this slutshaming and police themselves, and feel overwhelmed by the urge to overassess and correct themselves – from their behaviour and words to their outfits and lifestyle choices.

This is class-passing. We hear about the concept of passing in relation to gender and race, but it exists with class too. Often, class-passing is something that's done on purpose, as a means to get ahead. But sometimes it is more subtle than that and is done completely by accident. Some working-class people, often without realizing it, hide signifiers of their background, such as their accent, their clothing, details about their lives, even their word choices and the make-up they choose to wear, in order to 'pass' as a higher class.

One of Ghodsee's students created a fascinating study for her senior thesis that looks into how women use clothing to pass as upper class and increase their chances of having good relationships in middle-class environments like universities.

The researcher is from Hawaii, and she moved to Maine to start university at eighteen. She was stunned by how young women dressed there. It was completely different in New England than it was in Hawaii. They wore cashmere, pearl earrings, Barbour jackets and Hunter boots. 'It was a uniform of the upper class,' Ghodsee explains. 'By the second or third year, all the girls from working-class backgrounds, or outside of New England, tried to dress in this uniform so they could blend in, emulate the upper class and receive the same social benefits as them.'

Ghodsee tells me that this leaks into dating culture too. Upper-class men use class signifiers like clothing to identify women who belong to the same class group as them. Because this student grew up in Hawaii wearing shorts, flip-flops and tank tops, she didn't have the 'upper class uniform' and found herself being associated with poor women and therefore being deemed undateable.

But there are dangers to feeling like you have to conceal your background and your true identity. It can cause you to overfixate on what you are doing, saying and wearing, and this can be anxiety-inducing. Plus, changing who you are to be accepted in your environment can make you feel unwelcome, alone and unhappy. Using class-passing as a method to avoid slutshaming is just about surviving. But surviving isn't really living.

And no one should have to squash their identity to fit a mould that wasn't made for them in the first place.

Talking about classism

Conversations about class don't happen very often. It can feel icky to talk about money, and a lot of people are afraid of discussing social class openly because they will either be faced with their lack of privilege or have to admit they have an abundance of it.

It's important that we open these discussions up, though. Because if you're told over and over again that you're innately promiscuous, that your sexual freedom is causing a problem, that you're destined to be a bad parent and a bad partner, and that you're bringing the entire economy down with your sexuality, you can start to believe it.

Working-class women can, in a way, end up being gaslit into believing that they are everything the world says they are: chavs, sluts, freeloaders, of no real value to society.

Working-class or not, we will never know the full extent of anyone's sex life, especially not someone we don't know personally. It might be that a working-class woman you perceive as a slut *does* have a lot of consensual sex with multiple partners. And good for her! Either way, her sexual situation is not intrinsically linked with her social class, and she is deserving of your respect, empathy and ability to mind your damn business.

Ultimately, the solution to classism is ending capitalism, and that's a difficult feat.

Slutshaming across the class divide

Philosopher Fredric Jameson notoriously said it's easier to imagine the end of the world than the end of capitalism. But what we *can* do is free ourselves of capitalist, classist thinking in our day-to-day lives. We live in a world where transactional relationships are common. We're encouraged to foster relationships that can get us ahead, and abandon those that threaten our wealth and status.

Connection and community can help overcome classism, especially when it comes to slutshaming. And fostering genuine friendships and relationships can serve as a small but revolutionary act.

7.

How racism and slutshaming intertwine

Your experiences of sex are heavily influenced by your race, which means all our experiences of slutshaming will differ, depending on the colour of our skin. Slutshaming takes a different form when it happens to a woman of colour because they're

179

experiencing two forms of oppression – one for being a woman, and one for being a woman of colour.

We've seen how Taylor Swift has been slutshamed in the media for her past relationships. But when you compare the way she has been treated with artists like Nicki Minaj, Cardi B and Megan Thee Stallion, it's clear to see the added layer of racism when this happens to Black women.

Rapper, singer and songwriter Nicki Minaj was ruthlessly slutshamed for her notorious *Paper* magazine cover, captioned 'Minaj à Trois', which saw three images of Nicki posing in sexually suggestive positions, Photoshopped together, so she appeared to be grabbing her own breasts and licking her own inner thigh.

The Root magazine said the shoot 'upped the ante for celebrating Black women's sexuality', but as a result of it, Minaj was the subject of loaded sexual racism. She was compared to animals, told she was bringing shame on Black women and called 'trashy'. Swift, comparatively, while she is certainly shamed, has never been dehumanized or been used as a symbol to suggest that all white women are slutty because of her sexual activity.

Racism has a big part to play in slutshaming, and for the person on the receiving end, the psychological effects can weigh very heavily. To explore this, I'm bringing in other voices, as racist slutshaming is not something that relates to my personal experience. But I want to make it clear, as it's one of the most important messages of this whole book, that this section is for everyone, no matter the colour of your skin. Whether you're a victim of racist slutshaming, a perpetuator or a bystander, we all need to know how racism interacts with slutshaming so we can fight all its forms together.

How slutshaming and racism met

To understand how slutshaming and racism overlap, we have to look at the point where misogyny and racism met.

That point has a name: misogynoir. The term was coined in 2010 by gay Black feminist American academic Moya Bailey, who defined it 'to describe the particular brand of hatred directed at Black women in visual and popular culture'. Misogynoir includes the way Black women are uniquely slutshamed, and that started way back in racism's history.

Most of you will be aware of the slave trade (which is honestly a miracle because most Western schools *still* aren't legally required to include it in lesson plans), but you might not be aware of the role sex, sex shame and sexual exploitation played in controlling women of colour during this period and beyond.

In 'The Sexual Exploitation of Black Women from the Years 1619–2020', researcher Dominique R. Wilson says both Black men and women were sexually exploited during the slave trade, but Black women got it a lot worse. They were routinely assaulted and forced into pregnancies by slave owners. Slave owners justified their actions by pedalling the harmful stereotype that Black women were 'innately lustful beings', a stereotype that still persists today.

Mixed/Other author Natalie Morris has also spoken about this in her book. She says that women of colour, particularly Black women, are frequently fetishized because of their skin colour, hair texture and body shape. The 'difference' of women of colour is perceived by white people to be 'exotic', which leads to automatic assumptions about their sexual preferences and promiscuity.

This is something twenty-five-year-old Serena understands. She says, 'I've had guys on dating apps tell me they don't think they could handle me in the bedroom. I have not shared my sexual interests with them. There's nothing in my bio about this. When I ask them what makes them say this, they go silent.'

This specific brand of racist slutframing opens Black women up to sexual objectification and dehumanization, where the women are seen purely as an opportunity for a different kind of sex. 'You wouldn't believe how many guys have excitedly told me they've always wanted to sleep with a Black girl when we've just started talking,' Serena adds.

182

How racism and slutshaming intertwine

We mentioned the term 'jezebel' earlier in the book as a synonym for 'slut'. Dominique Wilson notes that this was traditionally a word reserved for Black women. His research outlines descriptive words associated with this stereotype: seductive, alluring, worldly, beguiling, tempting and lewd. While 'jezebel' was used as a stereotypical representation of Black women and a go-to insult, there has never been a synonym for 'slut' that specifically attacks a white woman.

And despite the deeply racist history of the word, 'jezebel' has stuck around. We hear Will Ferrell scream it at Margot Robbie in films as recent as *Barbie* (2023). And in a research paper entitled 'An American Tragedy: The Legacy of Slavery', researchers detail how Black women are still stereotyped as helplessly sexually promiscuous, especially those living in poor areas.

Sexual control was also used as a means to oppress Native Americans in the USA. The research paper 'Not an Indian Tradition: The Sexual Colonisation of Native Peoples' investigates the link between sexual violence and colonialism (when a country forcefully takes control over another country).

When Christopher Columbus invaded and took over America, Indigenous People were either killed, shipped off to other states, or mercilessly abused and forced to assimilate into Western society. They were made to speak English, dress in Western clothing and attend Christian-run Western schools. Part of this, the research reveals, involved forcing Western purity culture on to them.

Native Americans did not hold the same sexual values as the colonizers. Sexual shame wasn't a part of their culture. In fact, they were incredibly sexually open.

The Wendat people – one of the Indigenous communities in North America – didn't even have words in their language for 'shame', 'guilt' or 'innocence'. They celebrated female pleasure and entered relationships that closely resemble the kind of polyamorous lifestyles only just entering the mainstream around the world today.

You can imagine how Columbus and his mates took this. The Indigenous People's sexual openness was used as evidence of their 'animalistic' and 'savage' nature, and this was in turn used as justification for abuse. Soon, all the rules and restrictions of purity were forced on to Indigenous People who had no choice but to comply.

People often make the dangerous mistake of waving this racism off as a 'thing of the past', but the catastrophic racism throughout history – no matter how long ago these events were – continues to influence modern societies.

Researchers have shown in 'Girlhood Interrupted: The Erasure of Black Girls' Childhood' that Black girls are viewed through a hypersexual lens as a direct result of historical slavery. This has led to numerous myths about Black women: that they are promiscuous, or that they have a lot of children from different fathers. As a result of this, Black women are also much less likely to be believed when they report sexual assault, despite being most at risk of sexual violence.

As for Native American women, they are much more likely to go missing, be murdered or become victims of sexual violence than non-native Americans today. Some Indigenous communities are also rife with violent misogyny. Anthropologist John Steckley explains in his book *White Lies About the Inuit* how this was a direct impact of colonizers, who taught them patriarchy and misogynoir as a parting gift during the formation of the Indian Act – a bill passed in Canada in 1876 that saw the Canadian government gaining control of the native people's healthcare and housing.

It's crucial to take in this history and acknowledge where the increased levels of slutshaming that women of colour are up against have come from. With this knowledge, we can better understand the weight of words and stereotypes, and start moving away from the foundations they're built on. We can picture a way of living where women of colour aren't slutshamed simply for being who they are, and pave a path towards it.

Black women can't win

Black women have historically not been allowed the same access to sex as white women, or the same permissions to be explorative.

Dr Donna Oriowo is a sex and relationships therapist who leads an online community for Black women learning about racism and sexuality. On her Instagram she explores how white supremacy and patriarchy affect Black women's access to pleasure. 'Black folk – especially women – are penalised and deemed "deviant" for normal sexual exploration and body exploration of any kind,' she says.

Twenty-one-year-old university student Leah tells me she often feels jealous of her white friends when they go out clubbing, because she feels she can't be as 'sexually open' as they are in public. 'They basically run around looking for people to have sex with, and I just wish I could join in. We live in a predominantly white area. I went to an all-white school. I was the only Black girl there. I always feel like the official representative for all Black women,' she explains.

She adds that this comes with an enormous amount of pressure. 'Black women literally can't win. If I'm quiet, reserved and conservative, then I'm not acting like [white people's] idea of a Black girl and that makes them uncomfortable. If I'm loud and sexual and twerking all over the place, then I am fitting their idea of a Black girl and that also makes them uncomfortable,' she says.

Journalist Kayleigh Watson wrote an article for *gal-dem* magazine, discussing Chloe Bailey – American singer, songwriter and actress – who found herself subject to hateful slutshaming comments after

How racism and slutshaming intertwine

she had shared photos on Instagram that saw her exploring her femininity. Later, Bailey shared how the slut and bodyshaming comments had been affecting her. 'Whether a Black woman complies to or defies a sexual image, it appears they cannot win,' Watson wrote.

This type of slutshaming can also be seen in the treatment of model, rapper and television personality Amber Rose. In 2012, she was told in an interview by the host of the popular morning radio show *The Breakfast Club* that she should be 'seen and not heard' while being asked about her controversial love life. The implication behind this comment was that Rose was a slut, as the host was clearly hinting at her public sexual relationships.

For context, Amber Rose had two very public relationships with two American rappers, Kanye West and Wiz Khalifa, as well as other high-profile men.

Rose explains that she became part of the media's 'Hoe Hall of Fame'. In an interview with Charlie Brinkhurst-Cuff in *The New York Times*, she says she remembers 'feeling like I had to defend myself and who I dated, or who I didn't date, or who I had sex with'. Her public perception was not helped by myriad articles in the mainstream media documenting her relationships (whether they were confirmed or not), nor Kanye West's alleged comments that he had needed to 'take 30 showers' after they dated.

Rose also told Brinkhurst-Cuff that people seemed to believe she didn't deserve Kanye West and accused her of being a gold-digger. She adds that people threw things at her in the street while telling her so. To be verbally abused and have items thrown at you because of assumptions about your sexuality is abhorrent. It is a clear example of just how insidious racist slutshaming can be.

Dr Michele Leno, psychologist at DML Psychology Services in Michigan, USA, adds that it's not just Black women's behaviour that is policed. Often, Black women are shamed for their bodies for looking 'too sexual' (particularly voluptuous Black women).

Broadcaster, podcaster and writer Jackie Adedeji creates content on Instagram about bodyshaming, particularly when it comes to women who have big boobs. She tells me that, growing up, she often felt automatically slutshamed for having really big boobs, and because they were a natural part of her body, there was literally nothing she could do about it. Having a curvy body meant she was automatically looked at as a slut and vilified for it.

Adedeji adds that she looks similar to the fetishized fantasy of curvy Black women, and as a result she often notices how people seem to think it's OK to objectify her, slutshame her and dehumanize her.

How can Black women possibly win when their natural body shapes are weaponized against them?

How racism and slutshaming intertwine

Leno discusses how slutshaming can be emotionally distressing and draining for all women. 'The shamed woman may start to question her womanhood and do whatever it takes to fit in. She starts to feel less confident ... always second-guessing her appearance and behaviour in an effort to please the shamers,' she explains.

'You'll make us look bad'

Trauma is an emotional response to a horrifying event like an accident, violence or a natural disaster. Generational trauma is when the event is experienced by our ancestors, and they pass the emotional response down to the next generation.

Because Black women have historically been highly sexualized, objectified and then shamed for their sexual expression, some people in the community have internalized this slutshaming as a defence mechanism. They might police their sexuality to save themselves from scrutiny or abuse and pass this response on to their children. Who pass it on to their children. And so on.

They might tell their children and members of their wider family or community to cover up, to not dress in certain ways, to not sleep around. This kind of slutshaming within families and communities is actually very common in most marginalized groups. It's a defence mechanism performed by working-class people (see Chapter Six) and queer people (see Chapter Eight) as well, in order to try to prevent discrimination coming from outside of the community.

Adedeji shares that when you're Black, you're raised in a particular way. 'A lot of my Black friends grew up hearing "Don't do this" or "Don't act like that, you'll make us look bad."'

Adedeji says her dad, who is a pastor, has always had strong opinions about what she should wear. 'Just last year I wore a dress I thought was really covering for his birthday and in the family photo that we took that day we're all smiling, but what you can't see is my dad saying, "Why did you wear this dress? You are disgracing me" in my ear.'

Recently, Adedeji married her partner in an intimate ceremony in London, where her mother and pastor father walked her down the aisle. This was filmed, and while she was honeymooning in Paris she discovered her wedding had gone viral, but not for positive reasons.

Adedeji had worn a beautiful mini wedding dress. When Nigerian newspapers saw this, they picked it up as a news story. Soon she saw herself being slutshamed on TikTok, Instagram and across various news sites.

Nigerian newspaper *Pulse Nigeria* shared the video of her entrance into her ceremony to TikTok, with the caption: 'Church members in shock as pastor's daughter walks down the aisle in short dress.'

How racism and slutshaming intertwine

Comments included: 'So he corrected every child but their own', 'This could never be me' and 'our body should never be exposed like that', among others. Some even devalued Adedeji's father's position as a pastor and suggested he shouldn't be allowed to perform sermons or 'tell anyone anything' because of the way his daughter dressed.

In her Substack newsletter *More Than a Handful*, Adedeji writes about this experience, saying, 'I was on different Instagram pages, TikTok and Nigerian newspapers, and millions of people attacked me, my dress, those trusty space cowgirl boots and my bouquet. You name it, everything was up for grabs.'

She says she felt 'publicly bollocked by thousands' and that people were calling her a 'disgrace'. Even her mum started getting attacked by the public, and friends of the family, who originally said they'd liked her dress, appeared to change their minds and condemn her choice.

But she doesn't regret her outfit, not for a second. She writes, 'Despite everything that happened, I wouldn't change anything, because everything I wore I loved and enjoyed . . .'

Even if people's opinions make you want to hate your own decisions, don't. We give them too much power by giving in.

The promiscuity myth

Within the Black community, Black women are certainly slutshamed much more than men, but Black men don't get out unscathed.

The research paper 'The Myth of Promiscuity' examines the sexuality of Black men and identifies numerous common myths about them:

- Black men are promiscuous and therefore untrustworthy
- All Black men have huge penises, which means they are amazing at sex
- Black men are sexually experienced and offer otherwordly sex

In reality, these are all, of course, false and harmful stereotypes. Black men's penises come in all shapes and sizes, just like all other penises do. Black men are not all promiscuous, nor do they offer a specific type of sex because of the colour of their skin. They learn about sex through experimentation, trial and error, and terrible sex education lessons at school, just like everyone else!

Yet this myth that Black men are promiscuous is so ingrained that in the pornography industry it's been reported that white women avoid having sex with Black co-stars because it makes their white boyfriends jealous, or they're afraid they'll be considered a slut for having sex with Black men and even lose fans. These women are referred to as 'dodgers' by porn directors.

How racism and slutshaming intertwine

A quick scroll through Reddit shows how prevalent these pervasive myths are too. There are forums entirely dedicated to white men discussing whether or not they'd date a white woman who'd had sex with a Black man. A resounding 'no' is echoed by the majority of commenters.

Littered throughout the posts and comments is the idea that Black men are slutty, and white women who sleep with them are slutty by association. It is possible that these racist and misogynistic beliefs stem from historic adultery laws. In 1980s America, almost thirty years after the civil rights movement, there was still a huge issue of systemic racism in the country. And the arrival of adultery laws – criminalizing sexual affairs for married people – played into this.

Laws against cheating might seem like no big deal at first, but, in reality, they came with double standards. It was mostly women who were affected by these charges and what constituted cheating seemed to be subjective, highly political, and based on both patriarchal and racist ideas.

In 1955, a judge in North Carolina, USA, sent a woman named Janie Bell Weeks to jail for two years after she had been found guilty of adultery. But that's not exactly what the courts were really punishing her for. In an *Atlas Obscura* article, 'The Racist, Slut-Shaming History of Adultery Laws', it was reported that the crime that Weeks – who was white – was actually tried for was having sex with a Black man.

In practice, these laws were not just used to punish married people for sleeping around. They were used to enforce more specific social norms around sex and who, exactly, was allowed to sleep with whom. The same article reports that arrests for adultery overwhelmingly and suspiciously applied to Black men, and white women who slept with them, along with sex workers. A quote in the same article from JoAnne Sweeny, an associate law professor at the University of Louisville, suggests that race came up often in adultery cases of that era. 'In some of these older cases, in the 1930s, '40s, and '50s, they mention specifically if the person is black and the other person is white,' she says. 'You don't need to mention that, and they do.'

It's likely that these laws, and the harmful ways they were enforced, are a root of the racist myths and slutshaming that still persist today.

Islam and the invisible jury

Race and religion often intersect and create extra layers of complication for slutshaming. Muslim women, for instance, experience a very particular type of slutshaming that other women do not.

Shahed Ezaydi, journalist and author of *The Othered Woman: How White Feminism Harms Muslim Women*, tells me that young Muslim girls are not only having to deal with the same slutshaming

How racism and slutshaming intertwine

most women experience, but also with the unique way it overlaps with Islamophobia.

Some Muslim women might choose to wear hijabs, niqabs or shaylas, which cover certain parts of their heads, faces and bodies. Twenty-seven-year-old Aisha from New Jersey, USA, tells me, 'The practice originally came from the belief that women should cover up, but it's not about that any more. I wear a hijab because it connects me to my identity and it makes me feel empowered. It's not always about being pure or restrained. I have chosen to wear it because it makes me feel connected, focused and peaceful.'

Yet lots of people don't take the time to consider these nuances. Many Muslim women are 'prude-shamed' for their choice to cover up. Twenty-seven-year-old Fatima from Sheffield, UK, tells me she wears a hijab and has had others assume she is asexual as a result. She's also been left out of sexual conversations by people presuming she has no experience. And she says people automatically think she's being forced to wear modesty clothing, rather than it being her choice.

And often when Muslim women do make the choice to show skin, or not to wear any modesty clothing, they are slutshamed.

Fatima adds that young boys in her school would make horrible jokes about Muslim women being 'slutty' if they got their ankles or wrists out. 'I didn't wear a hijab while I was in school, but my mother did and it was heart-wrenching watching white boys make jokes about "dirty muslims getting their ankles out". It was like they didn't see it as racist because they didn't even see us as real people.'

Ezaydi explains that there is an unrelenting stereotype that Muslim women are without sexual agency and are simply passive and submissive. At the same time, Muslim women are also hyper-sexualized, especially if they wear modesty clothing, as people use their covering up as an invitation to speculate about what's beneath.

'These multiple racist imaginings trap women into prescribed sexual contexts,' Ezaydi says. They don't get to form their own sexual paths.

Because there's all this perceived mystery around Muslim girls and women's sexuality and what they're 'allowed' to do, there is a serious problem with young Muslim women being bullied in very specific and racist ways.

Ezaydi has had first-hand experience with this. 'I still remember when I was a teenager at school, I was nicknamed the "forbidden fruit" by some of the boys because I never had a boyfriend or anything. It made me feel weird and othered.'

In *gal-dem* magazine, Alya Mooro, author of *The Greater Freedom: Life as a Middle Eastern Woman Outside the Stereotypes*, says that

How racism and slutshaming intertwine

many Muslim and Middle Eastern women experience difficulty with feeling conflicted between two grapples of sexuality while living in the West. She says it can seem like there is an 'invisible jury' judging Muslim women, which they feel they must hold themselves to, that comes with this conflict. 'You are torn between two cultures and two moral compasses.'

It's important that in our fight against slutshaming we address racism, including Islamophobia. All women deserve to be saved from slutshaming.

Women of colour have rightly criticized the feminist movement for not always being inclusive of them, nor appreciating the cultural nuances that might bring conflict for women of certain races or religions when engaging with feminism. This is especially true when it comes to sex positivity and slutshaming, Ezaydi tells me. White-centric sex positivity isn't always mindful of the ways cultural and religious values like modesty might prohibit women from engaging in public acts of slut pride, for example.

We do have some way to go, but as conversations about intersectionality become more commonplace, feminism and sex positivity movements are becoming more inclusive of everyone. But we all have to make an effort to reach this place.

A number of safe, anti-slutshaming spaces have opened that are specifically for Black women. Leno explains that finding what makes you feel empowered and, more specifically, disconnected from racist slutshaming is key. Whether that's a workshop or joining an online community that fosters real acceptance, women can feel less alone and be armed to rebel against and let go of slutshaming in their own lives, if they find the spaces that work for them.

Inclusive Sex Positive Programmes

Black Women's Blueprint

Black Women's Blueprint is an organization that specifically addresses rape culture and sexual violence and its intersection with misogynoir. Their mission statement says they are there for 'the protection of Black women's sovereignty and dignity' and aim to empower 'Black women, girls and gender-fluid people to advocate for human rights and to secure gender and racial justice through the eradication of sexual violence'. They also offer a wide range of sexual health services for Black women.

Scotty Unfamous 'Best Heaux Life: Black Magic' Workshops

Influencer Scotty Unfamous, who has accumulated 19,400 followers on Instagram, creates regular content aimed at Black women. Her goal is to provide the representation she didn't have when she was younger in the sexual wellness space. Scotty's content includes everything from hilarious anecdotes about her sex life and

How racism and slutshaming intertwine

tangible sex tips you can take home to dispelling harmful myths and misconceptions about sex.

Scotty also hosts regular workshops titled 'Best Heaux Life: Black Magic', offering an intimate night of sharing sex tips and empowering Black people to carve out the sex lives they truly desire without shame. These workshops are hosted in London, but her online content is available worldwide.

Savage University

Run by Raquel Savage, a sex worker, educator and therapist, the Savage University is an archive of educational videos that includes guidance on how to unpack and address your own internalized slutshaming and whorephobia, and on how to craft a relationship with sex that works for you.

Savage created the hashtag #ThoughtProvokingThirstTraps. The idea is for people to post thirst traps (sexy selfies) with sex positive captions – highlighting discrimination in sex or celebrating your own personal joy with sex – which get audiences thinking. She also started a production company called Kink Media Group in 2020. Through this she posts her #SexxxEd series, a hands-on, informative and real-life version of sex ed aimed at adults who missed out on ethical and affirming sex education lessons growing up.

Ask Goody

Ask Goody is a website with a thriving Instagram community that offers sex positive advice, mantras and support for women of colour. Run by sex educator Goody Howard, www.askgoody.com also offers in-person workshops that focus on making sex better for you. She tours all over the USA with these workshops.

Free, Fabulous, and F*cked

Run by sex and relationships therapist Dr Oriowo, this is a sex positive community for women of colour across Instagram and Facebook. Users can access reliable psychological information about sex. Oriowo is also on Instagram herself, with a community of 6,500 followers, where she shares comprehensive information about the overlap between sex shame and racism, and how to let go of it.

The SlutWalk

SlutWalk is one initiative that's received a ton of worldwide praise for its inclusivity.

SlutWalk is a transnational rally, march, protest and movement aimed at raising awareness of rape culture, street harassment, sexual violence and victim-blaming.

It was started by five women in Toronto after police officer Michael Sanguinetti said 'women should avoid dressing like sluts in order not to be victimised' during a university visit,

How racism and slutshaming intertwine

during which he was supposed to be giving a talk about staying safe.

The first SlutWalk was a local one, in Toronto, with women wearing bikinis and dresses – the kind of slutty dressing we can presume Sanguinetti meant – and holding signs with messages like, 'Sluts against rape culture' and 'Met a slut today? Don't assault her.'

The initial protest prompted an apology from Sanguinetti, and the SlutWalk soon evolved from a single protest to an entire movement, aiming to dismantle rape culture. Since the first walk in 2011, SlutWalks have been organized in seventy-five cities across the world, from the USA and Canada to Sweden and South Africa. The *Washington Post* even reported in a 2011 op-ed by Jessica Valenti that in just a few months SlutWalks became 'the most successful feminist action of the past 20 years', stating that these protests and marches had created genuine change.

In the beginning, Black feminists were critical of the SlutWalk rallies because they centred on white women and excluded everybody else.

In a statement called 'An open letter from Black women to the SlutWalk', posted via Black Women's Blueprint, an organization dedicated to bringing Black voices into the rape culture discussion, multiple women of colour said that while they commended the organizers for calling out rape culture and doing something practical about it, it was white privilege which made it easier for white women to make moves like the SlutWalk.

One quote from the letter read, 'As Black women, we do not have the privilege or the space to call ourselves "slut" without validating the already historically entrenched ideology and recurring messages about what and who the Black woman is.

'We don't have the privilege to play on destructive representations burned in our collective minds, on our bodies and souls for generations.'

Some feminists of colour felt differently, though. In response, Janell Hobson, a Black women's studies professor and scholar at the University at Albany, State University of New York, also wrote an open letter in *Ms. Magazine*, expressing concern about the 'politics of respectability' that became a theme among SlutWalk critics – a sort of slutshaming within slutshaming.

She said, 'instead of seeking respectability, what would it mean to confront the danger of a word that was historically constructed to support economies of slavery and legal segregation? [. . .] I'd suggest that Black women, rather than oppose SlutWalk, should think of the ways it can be appropriated to serve our needs. I would like to see a SlutWalk with Black women front and centre.'

How racism and slutshaming intertwine

And eventually that happened. The white-centric nature of the SlutWalk changed drastically after the first rally in 2011. By 2013, the SlutWalk was taking place in many countries, with each protest being locally organized independently and without any overarching organization or control. This means the protests have taken many forms. In countries where it's dangerous to present as a slut, for example, SlutWalks have focused less on dressing as a slut to make a statement.

One research paper, 'The SlutWalk Movement: A Study in Transnational Feminist Activism', notes that in some countries women in nothing but bikinis have marched next to women in burkas, students marched alongside grandmothers and nuns, and significant numbers of men have participated in the events. Gay, lesbian and transgender people have been well represented in the marches too.

And the messages on the protestors' placards show that the intersection of slutshaming and racism is too important to ignore. One young Muslim woman doing a SlutWalk in a burka held a sign saying, 'My burka did not protect me from rape.'

Then, in 2015, Amber Rose organized her own culture-shifting SlutWalk in Los Angeles that would change conversations about slutshaming forever, showing that it was possible for women who looked like her to also proudly reclaim the word slut.

Kaitlynn Mendes, a professor of sociology at Western University in Ontario and the author of the book *SlutWalk: Feminism, Activism and Media*, attended Amber Rose's third SlutWalk in 2017 and told Brinkhurst-Cuff it was the most intersectional feminist event she had ever been to and the most diverse, crediting this achievement to the fact that a prominent woman of colour had organized it and held it in downtown Los Angeles, a very diverse area.

In the interview with Brinkhurst-Cuff, Rose boldly declares the SlutWalk 'going to battle' and I think these are important words to keep in mind as we interrogate and eradicate slutshaming for good.

Anti-slutshaming is not just popping on a T-shirt with 'slut' bedazzled across the chest or sharing a tongue-in-cheek meme about sex on Instagram. It should also be a battle, and we should fight for every single woman who has been hurt by slutshaming, not just ourselves. It will be difficult, but that's because it matters.

8.

Slutshaming in the queer community

It's 2018 and I'm organizing a lunch in my office for Spirit Day, an annual LGBTQ+ awareness day usually observed in October to raise awareness of homophobic bullying in schools around the world. The day is connected to the suicide of a young schoolchild, who ended their life after homophobic harassment. I've made a purple cake (the colour used across the globe to mark this occasion) and set it on the table in the communal kitchen.

My colleagues were mainly straight tech bros at the time, and as the LGBTQ+ office representative it was my job to do events like these. As part of my role, I was responsible for improving LGBTQ+ diversity in the office, raising awareness about issues faced by the community and answering anyone's questions about LGBTQ+ topics.

On that day, I was expecting questions about Spirit Day's history, but instead a colleague asked me loaded questions about why I care about the day and why he should have to care as well. When I explained that I was bisexual and cared a lot about schoolchildren being bullied for being gay, his response was sympathy, but not for me or the vulnerable gay children for whom the day was supposed to be about.

'Wow, your poor boyfriend,' he said instead.

I should have walked away, but the journalist (read: nosy person) in me had to know what was making him so hateful, so I asked him what he meant.

'There's no way I could go out with a bisexual woman. I'd always worry they're fucking around or they're going to go back to women,' he explained. 'Would be good for threesomes, though,' he admitted, generating a laugh from other surrounding tech bros.

Slutshaming in the queer community

This conversation was horrifying for myriad reasons. It happened in the most inappropriate environment imaginable (the workplace), and he had degraded an important and serious occasion. But mostly I felt unsafe. The assumption that I was a slut because I was bisexual, and that he found me undateable because of this, and believed my partner should too, was scary.

Did my partner fear I was shagging left, right and centre every time I left the house? Did people look at us and think he was with someone dirty? Would he eventually leave me?

This conversation is one of many experiences I've had of queer slutshaming. And it's something most people in the LGBTQ+ community will unfortunately likely be familiar with too.

Queer people are often the victim of assumptions, whether that's about having a lot of sexual partners or catching a lot of STIs. And this can lead to some seriously harmful incidents of slutshaming. So, we're going to look at where this stems from, learn the historical context behind queer stereotyping (because, *boy*, have the '80s got a lot to answer for), and understand how we can combat the grim combo deal literally no one asked for: homophobic slutshaming.

An excuse to slut around

Often, it's felt as though my bisexuality has either been a problem or a win in the dating world, with no in between. Whether you're male or female, being a bisexual person (someone who is attracted to all genders) or a pansexual person (someone who is attracted to people regardless of gender) comes with the unique experience of either being fetishized or despised. Many bisexual women, for instance, report struggling to date lesbian women because they are frequently faced with assumptions that they are promiscuous or greedy, and that they won't make good partners. While on the other side, when people are happy to date a bisexual person, they often make objectifying assumptions about what they will be like in bed and the potential for regular threesomes.

When dating straight men, what happens a lot is bisexual women are initially fetishized by them, only to be oppressed by them later on. Twenty-nine-year-old Poppy* from Wolverhampton, UK, tells me that when she was on a dating app last year she got a lot of attention from straight men who seemed excited that her bio said she was bisexual. But when dating app conversations turned into dates and dates turned into the beginnings of romantic relationships, things started to go wrong.

These men would suddenly want her bisexuality to disappear. They'd say things like, 'Well, you're straight now, because you're with me,' or ask her not to mention ex-girlfriends, or anything else that would 'give her away' around their other guy friends or their family. And some were scared she would suddenly start thinking about girls again and cheat on them.

Twenty-nine-year-old drag queen Chris* from New York, USA, is also bisexual and tells me he prefers to date women. But when he tells straight women that he's bisexual, they are often cold or even cruel to him, and there's always a tone of slutshaming involved. On a recent date, he told the woman that he'd just got out of a relationship with a man. She stiffened, horrified that he had slept with men before.

Chris also says he's received plenty of 'jokes' about being greedy, and many people explicitly call him a slut when they find out he's bi.

'It's so normalized to slutshame bisexual people, they don't even hide it in humour, it's just there. You're *allowed* to say it. It's exhausting,' Chris says.

In 'From Bias to Bisexual Health Disparities: Attitudes toward Bisexual Men and Women in the USA', sex researcher Brian Dodge found that bisexuals are slutshamed and, as a result, are often actively avoided by people who are seeking sexual or romantic partners. The research uncovered how this avoidance is also because straight people generally believe that having sex or a relationship with a bisexual person places an 'unwanted bridge between them and homosexuals'. Since some bisexual people will have sex with both straight and queer people, they worry that bisexuals could 'pass their sexual behaviour on to them'.

So, straight people generally think sexual behaviour is contagious. And they think homosexuals are having sex like this:

- At a much younger age
- With much older people
- With more sexual partners
- Contracting STIs left, right and centre

Because people believe in these harmful assumptions about the sluttiness of homosexual people, and that this sluttiness is contagious, many subscribe to the idea that bisexuals (who are open to sleeping with gay and straight people) are the ultimate, most contagious of sluts.

This study also found that straight people connect sleeping with bisexual people with entering the same sexual 'pool' as 'fully gay' people, and therefore run the risk of contracting STIs (due to those stereotypes).

As a result of these many harmful assumptions, queer women often feel like they can't truly be themselves in romantic relationships. In fact, a recent study in the *Journal of Bisexuality* found that bisexual women with straight male partners were actually the least likely to be 'out'.

And bisexual men experience this slutshaming too. Twenty-six-year-old copywriter George* from London, UK, tells me he was recently 'very bluntly' rejected on a first date with a guy he'd been talking to on the dating app Hinge after he said he was bisexual. The guy said he'd been 'burnt by bisexuals before' and had no interest in being someone's 'just for now' partner.

'It never used to bother me, the whole "bisexual slut" stereotype, but that one hurt. I literally just want to be loved.'

Slutshaming comments like this can live in your brain for a long time, leaving you with internalized shame that's hard to overcome. And when that shame is attached to your sexuality, and thus your identity, it's all the more pervasive. It can affect your social life, sex life and dating success.

The statistics illustrate this too: a report on queer dating from Hinge showed that compared to other LGBTQIA+ daters, bisexual people in the UK are three times more likely to have never had a queer dating experience. They fear exploring dating with the same sex, partly because they fear being shamed by 'fully gay' people.

Bisexuality (and pansexuality by extension) is commonly viewed as a sexuality that isn't real in the first place. Multiple studies show that many people believe bisexuality is not genuine, and that it's used merely as an excuse to 'slut around'. For bisexual daters, it can be even more intimidating to disclose it's their first time due to the fear of biphobia they might experience. Often, bisexuals will default to dating 'straight' and concealing their queerness for survival, but no one should ever have to restrict who they fall in love or lust with, just to make it through the day. When it comes to love and sex, we all deserve abundance.

HIV and the new wave of slutshaming

This fear around bisexuals bridging homosexuality and heterosexuality and getting their slutty paws on everyone is deeply rooted in huge misunderstandings about HIV. In 1981, Human immunodeficiency virus (HIV) wreaked havoc across the world. It is a virus that attacks the body's natural immune system and weakens its ability to fight off disease and infection. It started in Central Africa, then arrived in America and Sweden with the first cases being reported in the summer of 1981. Later that winter, it reached Europe, before it was officially declared an epidemic by the World Health Organization. It is still ongoing today. HIV was and still is more common in gay men, who are twenty-five times more likely to contract the virus.

This is because the chance of transmission is higher during anal sex without a condom than vaginal sex without a condom. At the

Slutshaming in the queer community

time, anal sex was more likely to be practised by queer men. And, in general, using condoms during sex was not common before HIV's arrival, not even with new sexual partners.

In the 1980s, 100,777 people in the USA died from AIDS (a life-threatening disease HIV can develop into if left untreated or diagnosed too late). The statistics for the UK are unclear, but forty-two people had died of AIDS by 1984, according to parliament records, and the death toll peaked in 1995 when more than 1,700 people lost their lives.

Worldwide, approximately 6,400,000 people had died from AIDS by 1995, according to the Centers for Disease Control and Prevention. By 1991, World Health Organization statistics showed that a whopping 10 million people had HIV across the world.

It certainly wasn't impossible for straight people to catch HIV. That happened. But the media narrative was that it was a gay man's disease. So you can only imagine how HIV transformed from a health emergency into moral panic about gay men's sexual promiscuity.

Soon, public health campaigns hit TV screens across the world, sharing some wild assumptions and packed with slutshaming myths, such as the idea that having sex with a lot of people automatically increased your chances of disease (correction: if you're practising safe sex, this is not the case). And, in true purity culture style, for the most part, they also unhelpfully chose to endorse celibacy or monogamy rather than educating people about risk-management and safer sex.

In the USA, a public health campaign video was released in which promiscuity was presented as the ultimate cause of AIDS. The penis was represented by a gun and the infected semen by killer bullets. This associated HIV transmission, which in most cases was unintentional, with murder. The implication? Those who have free sex are knowingly going head-first into a danger zone and deserve whatever consequences come their way.

An image published in the popular science magazine *Discover* in 1985 included illustrated myths about human anatomy. It portrayed the rectum as 'vulnerable' and the vagina as 'rugged . . . designated to withstand the trauma of intercourse'. As a result, the article concluded, 'AIDS . . . is now – and is likely to remain – largely the fatal price one can pay for anal intercourse.'

Some countries were praised for their public health campaign efforts, though – particularly Australia, whose adverts focused on safety and addressing the very real risks, rather than spreading unhelpful myths about queerness. Their most notorious advert during the HIV epidemic was 'The Grim Reaper national' in 1987, which was a TV advert showing the grim reaper taking men, women and children away to die because they had AIDS. The script explicitly said that it was not only a gay issue but everyone's issue: 'soon AIDS will kill more people than World War Two', it announced. While it had its critics for how frightening it was, it's still praised today by experts in the HIV space for encouraging people to take safe sex seriously by including the quote, 'Have sex with one partner or always use a condom. Always.' It also made HIV everyone's problem to battle, not just gay men's.

A similar campaign was then played on television in the UK and Europe in 1987 called 'Don't Die of Ignorance', which featured frightening images of a giant gravestone with 'AIDS' written across it being built, then falling to the ground. 'If you ignore AIDS, it could kill you. Don't die of ignorance,' it said.

Sex educator Erica Smith tells me about another public health campaign in America at the time – the 'sexual exposure chart'. It was used as a way to deter people from having casual, unprotected sex during the crisis. The sexual exposure chart warns the beholder that if you have sex with a person, you're having sex with everyone they've ever had sex with as well. It says that if you've had ten partners, and your partners also have had ten partners, you'll be exposed to more than 1,000 people, who you'll also be having sex with.

She says, 'It might seem like a positive thing to encourage people to think about where other people have been during a time of mass disease spreading, but there was so much misinformation about HIV and about how gay people have sex, and this chart is full of such misinformation.' It also reinforces the dangerous myths of purity culture, including the idea that you're permanently tainted by everyone you sleep with and everyone they have slept with too.

Yet, Smith tells me this chart is still used in American, British and European classrooms today. It means more than forty years after the epidemic, those harmful stereotypes that permeated throughout the world are continuing to impact our education systems. Surely a better idea would be to tell young people that no number of sexual partners is shameful, and instead teach them important lessons about contraception, STIs and other harm-reduction methods?

In response to this, some empowering and inclusive queer-friendly organizations and institutions have popped up in recent years, with the aim of spreading more helpful information and sex education.

Ruby Rare

Sex educator and influencer Ruby Rare frequently facilitates workshops on her platform, showing people how to talk about gay sex *without* the slutshaming misconceptions. She tells me that queer sex is missing from sex education in schools (I will be talking more about this later in the chapter) and this creates an 'unknownness' that makes sex feel scary for LGBTQ+ people.

Ruby also aims her queer sex education at those who are opposing it, such as those who are against transgender rights. She says she tries to approach these people with softness. 'I like to work out where their fear is coming from. For some people (not everyone) that fear is coming from a place of care. For those people, educating them about transgender young people and their identities can help take that fear away.' She adds that a lot of people opposing LGBTQ+ sex education say they are worried about 'protecting children', so she carefully explains how accurate and inclusive sex education does precisely that.

Terrence Higgins

The Terrence Higgins Trust is a British charity committed to ending HIV. Part of that mission is investigating the quality of LGBTQ+ sex education in the UK to identify areas for improvement, so we can make schools better for young queer people.

They now say that the stigma surrounding HIV – the one that says men with HIV are inherently slutty, dirty and contagious – is more dangerous than the disease itself.

In 2023, the first health advert about HIV (since the 'Don't Die of Ignorance' campaign) aired on televisions in Scotland. Called 'Stigma is More Harmful', executives from the Terrence Higgins Trust say they created it 'based on the direct experiences of people living with HIV in Scotland who shared how much of a challenge the stigma still surrounding HIV is in their day-to-day lives'.

'[. . .] alongside all the good news about HIV today, we knew we had to show how devastating HIV-related stigma can be for those directly impacted,' they added.

The film, which aired on 16 October 2023, is a welcome and necessary change, with Jenni Minto, the public health minister for the Scottish government, admitting the campaigns of the 1980s 'have left a damaging legacy of stereotypes'. Hopefully more films like this can be broadcast across the world.

It Gets Better Project

The mission for the It Gets Better Project is to uplift, empower and connect LGBTQ+ youth around the globe. One of their services is providing support and resources for better queer-inclusive sex education. They offer comprehensive advice, guides and even assignments to both teachers and students.

PrEP whores

PrEP is one of the best inventions to ever grace this earth. In fact, it's so brilliant that I can't believe we don't have weekly parades celebrating its arrival. Yet somehow slutshaming manages to sneak its way into discussions about it.

A revolution in the HIV and AIDS crisis, pre-exposure prophylaxis (PrEP) was approved for use in the UK and the USA in 2012, the EU in 2016 and Australia in 2018. Intended to be taken by those who may come into sexual contact with someone who could have HIV, PrEP prevents users from contracting the virus, reducing the risk of it being passed on by ninety-nine per cent.

You'd imagine that the discourse around PrEP would be overwhelmingly positive. I mean, a tiny little pill can single-handedly prevent the transmission of one of the most frightening diseases in history. It's a big deal. But the arrival of the medication unfortunately birthed a new type of slutshaming. (Because we needed more of that!)

Enter: PrEP-shaming.

In the 2016 research paper 'PrEP Whores and HIV Prevention: The Queer Communication of HIV Pre-Exposure Prophylaxis (PrEP)', researchers found that the arrival of PrEP created a new category of queer people: the 'PrEP whores'. People who take PrEP are frequently painted as sluts and shamed for doing so.

FS magazine, a publication by Gay Men Fighting Aids, released a report in 2018 showing that roughly thirty-three per cent of men on the drug have experienced discrimination over taking PrEP in the UK. The discovery follows similar trends in the USA, where men on PrEP have also reported ridicule over the drug regimen. Forty-three per cent of men on PrEP were called a slut specifically because they were taking the medication.

The slutshaming around PrEP has the potential to overshadow its scientific accomplishment and even 'cloud the judgement of medical providers, policymakers, insurers and potential PrEP users', according to the 'PrEP Whores' research. Essentially, the availability of PrEP could be affected by the slutshaming that surrounds it, as lawmakers and governing bodies could deem it a 'dirty' device for promiscuity and see it as less of a priority.

This is something twenty-eight-year-old Amanda has experienced first-hand. 'My boyfriend's bisexual and we're in a polyamorous relationship, so it was for the best that we both started taking PrEP,' she tells me. 'But I was slutshamed by a doctor when I asked for it. He implied I don't use condoms, and sarcastically asked me if I've ever heard of them. He then told me that having less sexual partners is always the best way to reduce STIs.' Amanda couldn't believe what she had to go through to get the medication she needed.

PrEP is already facing shortage problems in some areas of the UK, Ireland, mainland Europe, the USA, Australia and New Zealand. It's also not available in some countries, even where homosexuality is legal, including Japan. In fact, only sixteen out of the fifty-three countries offering PrEP do so through a national health service, which would make it free to access. Yet this medication is so important for protecting queer people who are at risk of contracting or passing on HIV.

Slutshaming in the queer community

Ian Howley, chief executive of Health Equality and Rights Organisation (HERO), said of the survey on PrEP users, 'We really need to stop slutshaming each other. Calling each other lazy, irresponsible or promiscuous does nothing to stop the spread of HIV. It only takes one sexual encounter for HIV and STIs to be passed on.'

He added, 'Those who are on PrEP are being responsible. They are stopping the spread of HIV within the gay and bisexual communities. We should be applauding them, not shaming them.'

Legislating sex hate

Stepping back a few years to during the HIV epidemic and its aftermath, an irrational fear and hatred of queer people was rippling across the world, more so than ever before. In 1988, the then UK prime minister, Margaret Thatcher, and her Conservative government enacted Section 28, a cruel, ambiguous and confused piece of legislation that prohibited the 'promotion of homosexuality' by local authorities. It's thought to have been inspired by the Hays Code in America, which banned the representation of homosexuality (among other things) in Hollywood films from the 1930s until the 1960s.

Section 28 prevented teachers from mentioning queer relationships in sex education classes, and led to the removal of LGBTQ+ texts from schools, libraries and other institutions. Author and professor

Paul Baker, in an interview with *Dazed and Confused* magazine, said that anti-gay campaigners at the time were spreading the highly misleading idea that 'loony left' Labour councils were trying to 'teach' gay sex in schools.

This moral panic was fuelled by myths about gay promiscuity and the idea that queer people were sleeping around with multiple partners to a dangerous degree. A 1989 study into 'gay male promiscuity' reported that it was common for participants to have more than one hundred sexual partners. It was later found that researchers were purposely overpopulating their research pool with 'promiscuous respondents', so the results were unreliable. Even today, studies into queer sexual behaviour are overwhelmingly built through questionnaires given out in environments that attract slutty people, such as on Grindr – an app literally designed to provide easy hook-ups for queer people.

An extensive 1994 study, however, that used a fair, representative sample, found that the difference in the average number of sexual partners between gay and straight men 'did not appear very large'. In other words, the whole 'all gay men are sluts' thing is completely unfounded.

Section 28 was finally repealed in 2003, but if the panicked cries of 'Oh god, gay men are being overtly sexual! They're a danger to children and society itself!' sound eerily familiar, it's because a similar type of moral panic is being applied to transgender people now.

As I write this in 2023, stories about transgender people are featured heavily in British national newspapers, and on Australian and American news channels, and they are rarely portrayed in a positive light. A recurring theme, both in traditional media outlets and on social media, is that idea that transgender people are innately sexual, and that they represent and encourage sex. They are therefore presented as a danger to children.

According to Mermaids, a UK-based charity that supports transgender, non-binary and gender-diverse children, over the last six years the British press has increased its coverage of stories about trans people, writing roughly three and a half times as many articles in 2018–19 compared to 2012. But the organization found that transgender people are often described as 'exotic figures of entertainment' in the media and usually mis-described as 'transexual' – almost as if they're desperate to get the word 'sex' in there. Other articles condemn them for 'inappropriate clothing'.

Mermaids also note that it was rare to see transgender people in film and TV up until very recently. The most common job assigned to fictional transgender characters is sex worker.

These representations have serious effects. As transgender hate in the media has increased over the last few years, so has the number of transgender hate crimes. Trans women frequently report being sexually harassed online and assumed to be sex workers. And transgender people are also now four times more likely to be the victim of a sex crime compared with cisgender women.

In 2021, 2,630 hate crimes against transgender people were recorded by the police in the UK, an increase of sixteen per cent from the previous year, according to the Home Office. And according to charity Stop Hate UK, this number is still severely under-reported because out of 108,100 responses to the National LGBT Survey, eighty-eight per cent of transgender people said they did not report the most serious incidents they had been victims of.

In America, the situation worsens. Heartbreakingly, 2022 saw forty transgender and non-conforming people fatally shot in transphobic attacks. In Australia, a 2023 report found that half of transgender Australians experienced some form of hate within the preceding year.

The European Union Agency for Fundamental Rights has also shared on its website that transphobic hate crimes in the European Union have hit an all-time high. A project of TGEU (Transgender Europe) maps murders of trans people across the world. In 2022, it reported more than 320 trans people had been murdered. Most of them were Black trans women. In Europe, a third of those murdered were migrants. Unfortunately, the European Union also admit that they do not have comprehensive, recent data on exactly how many transgender people experience hate crime and in what capacity. This changed in 2023, though, with the introduction of an open survey for LGBTQ+ people to share their experiences. This is crucial in order to see the magnitude of the problem, and to counter violence against and harassment of LGBTQIA+ people.

At the root of this hate is an idea that transgender people are naturally and dangerously promiscuous and sometimes even perverted. Though it might not seem obvious at first, this slutshaming of transgender people is everywhere – even in our celebrity culture.

In 2019 British singer Sam Smith came out to the public as non-binary, using they/them pronouns. The way the mainstream media reacted, you'd think Smith announced they kick kittens for fun.

In an Apple Music interview with Zane Lowe, Smith said that after coming out they were abused both online and in the street. The media and the public used Sam's transition to criticize them, discredit their talent and oversexualize them.

In an article in *Spiked*, journalist Brendan O'Neill referred to the way Sam expressed their identity as a 'kink' and wrote that we should 'bring back kink shaming'. The article rips apart Sam's identity, their appearance and their perceived promiscuity. Only then does O'Neill jump into what he clearly aimed to write in the first place: why he believes pronouns – and gender non-conforming identities in general – are not valid.

This kind of transphobic slutshaming has a serious impact. In 2023, British Prime Minister Rishi Sunak delivered a speech at the Conservative Party press conference that featured a lot of transphobia. He said, 'Men are men and women are women, that's just common sense,' before suggesting children were being taught otherwise in sex education. He promised to work on censoring this and allowing parents to have a say in whether their children receive sex education at all. Considering how important we now know inclusive sex education is for combatting slutshaming, rape culture and homophobia, this is really worrying.

This idea – which, at the time of writing, has not yet come into legislation – feels like an echo of Section 28, and the UK isn't alone. Inclusion of transgender education in sex education has also been vilified by senators in the USA, despite only seventeen states including gender identity lessons in their sex education curriculum.

In 2022, legislation remarkably similar to Section 28 was applied in multiple states of America. Florida also enacted a bill formally know as the 'Parental Rights in Action' bill, but dubbed by critics with the incredibly on-the-nose name 'Don't Say Gay', which bans LGBTQ+ topics from being discussed in classrooms, either by school staff or third parties, between kindergarten and third grade.

After third grade, these topics must be 'age appropriate', however the bill does not define this term.

Poland has also enacted similar legislation, while Hungary has a long-standing anti-LGBTQ+ law similar to that of Section 28. In 2021, they brought in a bill to 'ban the popularisation of sexual deviancy' drafted by former member of the National Assembly of Hungary, Ádám Mirkóczki. This was to target 'homosexuality, sex changes, transvestitism, bisexuality and paedophile behaviour'.

It's so important to remember how stereotypes about queer people in the '80s translated into law and significantly damaged the community. And there's always a chance it could happen again before homophobia – and slutshaming – are eradicated. Our progress as a community has not been linear, and while I definitely encourage celebrating moments of freedom, the key is to acknowledge how fragile liberation is and remember that the fight isn't over. We still have work to do, especially for transgender people.

Making positive change

So how can we help make these important changes? Despite all the scary homophobia and transphobia in the world, there's still so much joy to be found in being authentically yourself, and this in itself can be a revolutionary act.

In the same Apple Music interview, Smith shared that they have experienced 'joy in abundance' since coming out as non-binary and being more themselves. Who is anyone to try to take that amazing experience away?

There are things we can do to ensure the world is a shame-free and safe space for everyone to experience joy in abundance:

- Remember that to fight slutshaming you have to consider the marginalized groups who experience slutshaming in a different way, including all LBGTQIA+ people
- Don't laugh off other people's jokes or remarks about LGBTQIA+ people, especially if they're sexualized. Call them out or call them in to help them understand the true impact of slutshaming people in this way
- Call out newspapers and outlets who slutshame LGBTQIA+ people by leaving comments or writing to them directly (and to Ofcom)
- Prise the right-wing newspapers from your nan's hands if you have to!

Why queer people slutshame each other

If you are queer, you'll know that slutshaming is a pretty common problem within the community. If you're not queer, hi. Welcome. Slutshaming is a big problem within the community!

Slutshaming in the queer community

With all this history of discrimination against queer people, you'd think we'd avoid slutshaming one another. But whether you're gay, bi, lesbian, transgender, non-binary or one of the other many letters in the gay alphabet (LGBTQIAA+), casual slutshaming is rife.

It might be that slutshaming is so prevalent in your life that you don't even notice it as a *thing*. So often, slutshaming simply lurks stealthily in the background while we socialize.

A lot of queer people point out the strange double standards around sexual behaviour in their community. Silva Neves, a sex and relationships psychotherapist who specializes in LGBTQ+ topics, says that, on the one hand, it is, in fact, a statement of pride to own being a slut among queer people. The gay scene is sexualized in many ways to respond to years of oppression, and open sexual expression is a way to celebrate your identity.

But on the other hand, there's serious internalized homophobia and slutshaming in the queer community that often goes unaddressed. Neves tells me that it's because there is such a widespread stereotype that all gay men are sluts, that gay men are so prone to slutshaming each other. In other words, queer men may slutshame one another to correct behaviour that might trigger discrimination from outside groups. In a way, it is slutshaming as a defence mechanism for . . . slutshaming.

Neves explains that gay men are therefore caught between internalized homophobia (from society) and the pressure to be overtly sexual (by the gay scene standards).

However, in a 2014 article published in the *Journal of Adolescent Research*, Drs McDavitt and Mutchler examined what prompts and prevents sexual communication between queer people. They conducted extensive interviews with participants aged between eighteen and twenty-one to better understand how young gay men communicate with their friends and how slutshaming manifests in day-to-day conversation.

The researchers noted that calling a friend a 'slut' or a similar word could actually result in 'playfully judgemental' talk. They mean the tongue-in-cheek 'hoe' you say to your friend, elbowing them as they leave the bar with a guy. Or the 'slut' you shoot your friend when she's had several shots during a game of Never Have I Ever.

Researchers say that sometimes casual slutshaming in the queer community is like a comfort blanket. Conversations about sex can be awkward and difficult, especially if your community has been shamed about sex for decades, and slutshaming each other creates a playful sex dialogue. For some, it's the antidote to anxiety around sex chat. Essentially, for a long time, queer sex (especially gay male sexuality) carried heavy connotations of HIV and death, which came along with shame, isolation and pain that was difficult to avoid, and some still experience this today. McDavitt and Mutchler believe slutshaming in the queer community is sometimes a way for gay men to promote fun conversations about casual or anonymous sex to make them seem less scary.

It could also be a way for gay men to discuss their sexuality in general. Purity culture prevents most of us, to some extent, from speaking freely about sex. Women have created their own pockets of freedom through sleepovers and group chats and drunken conversations in nightclub toilets. Yet there's not really an equivalent for men. So, researchers theorize that gay men, who may yearn for this sort of dialogue and outlet, introduce slutshaming into their friendships to talk about sex in general.

On this occasion, slutshaming – only in this playful form – becomes an important outlet for queer people to celebrate themselves and express their freedom.

Slutshaming queer people is never really about queer people, no matter who it's coming from. Florence Schechter, biochemist, founder of the Vagina Museum in London, UK, and author of *V: An empowering celebration of the vulva and vagina,* beautifully sums up why the slutshaming of queer people is so deeply ingrained. 'To be queer is to have subverted gender, which undermines the patriarchy, particularly if you're a queer woman. To be gay is to [subvert from] gender (and gender roles) so the patriarchy works harder in slutshaming you.'

This is why queer people are so often described as 'shameless' in a derogatory way. It serves as a reminder that we are expected to feel ashamed about our sex. But being shameless is the entire point of great, pleasurable sex.

Being a queer slut is about finding joy in sexual experiences *despite* the shame being thrown our way. Shame doesn't belong in the bedroom, no matter how hard it tries to snake its way in. Being 'shameless' in sex is something to aspire to, not look down on.

9.

The true consequences of slutshaming

Horrifying fact incoming: did you know that the experience of slutshaming can live inside your body? Along with the purity culture it stems from, slutshaming can wiggle into the brain and the body like a parasite.

Even when we don't personally agree with the messaging, it can impact things like our sexual pleasure and our desire to experiment sexually, because deeply embedded somewhere in our minds are the ideas that this is wrong.

Silva Neves, a sex and relationships psychotherapist who specializes in LGBTQ+ topics, explains that this influence can go even further. Fifty-two per cent of people with penises experience erectile dysfunction, while forty-three per cent of women and thirty-one per cent of men struggle with a lack of arousal. And this could be caused by slutshaming. Our brains communicate directly with our genitals. So, when it comes to having sex, if we have absorbed slutshaming messages at some point in our lives, this can cause our brain to make a bit of a mistake. It might signal to the genitals that something is wrong (because slutshaming culture has told us that sexual pleasure is wrong), which creates a response in the genitals to shut things down. It's kind of like a fight-or-flight response for the penis or vagina.

Essentially, not only does slutshaming make us feel, well, ashamed, but it can even cause sexual dysfunction.

This is important as both Neves and Michael Yates, a clinical psychologist specializing in sexual issues from The Havelock Clinic, tell me that they see hundreds of patients at their clinics who think they are 'broken' because of sexual dysfunction, and it's usually nothing to do with their bodies. It can be, of course, but most of the time, it's psychological. Ninety per cent of all vaginismus cases are due to psychological causes according to the

The true consequences of slutshaming

Vaginismus Center, along with forty per cent of erectile dysfunction cases. Neves and Yates both agree that, for some people, this is because they believe in purity culture myths, or have been slutshamed and that shame is living in the body.

Yates says there are ways to release it, though. He recommends working out your own sexual values, without the noise and influences of our slutshaming society. He advises setting your own trajectory around sex. Think of it like making a five-year plan, but for your sex life.

Ask yourself:

- **What are my values/opinions about sex that are important to me personally?** For example, perhaps it's that each person should be the expert of their own body and know how it works, what it looks like and how it feels.
- **How do these values work for me?** Maybe you're much more comfortable with sex when you have a lot of knowledge about it, so being an expert in your body makes sex better.
- **What do I want my ideal sex life to look like?** Adventurous and spontaneous, or scheduled and planned out, or a mixture.
- **How would I like to express myself sexually?** Hugging/cuddling, kissing, sexual touching, sexual penetration, being open to a variety of acts and experimenting with

different techniques, or being more reserved and wanting to stay in your comfort zone.

- **How would I like to treat others with regard to sex?** For example, warm, welcoming, helpful, advice-giving.
- **What do I want to be?** Adventurous, compassionate, open . . .

It can help to temporarily mute outside influences, such as social media. This way, you can properly self-reflect and decipher what you truly want from sex, rather than what everyone else expects you to want. Then you can create your own personal sexual trajectory.

I did this exercise myself by taking a social media break for a week, heading to the park with a notepad and paper, and answering these important questions. In case it helps you, here are my answers:

- My values are that as long as sex is consensual, safe and fun, any and all sex has value, and that everyone should understand, respect and take care of their own bodies and that of their partners. I also believe that no one should ever be shamed for their sexual preferences, and their sexual history has nothing to do with their ability to be a good partner.
- These work for me because I've found that physical intimacy is important in order to feel pleasure and connection to my

body. This was especially important having experienced a lot of not-so-great sex throughout my life and struggling with shame.

- Ideally, I'd like my sex life to be happy – to contain genuine joy and be focused on mutual pleasure.
- In terms of sexual expression, I want to be free, whether that's on my own or with a partner. I want to have the sex I fantasize about without questioning my behaviour or worrying about what others might think. I want to be someone who my partner can talk to about their fantasies too. I want my sex to include penetrative sex, but also oral and hand sex, which is just as important to me. I want to centre my sex life around physical touch rather than focusing on penetration, so kissing, cuddling – simply touching – is just as important.
- I want to be the kind of person who friends come to when they want advice about sex, and I want to foster a kind space where no one feels shame when they ask me anything about sex, no matter how 'weird' it is. I want to treat others with non-judgemental care and support, and help them be safe and keep their excitement and curiosity up.
- I want to be open to new sexual ideas, adventurous with myself and my partner, and be kind to myself, my partners and others about their sexual expression too.

Having a clear destination like this to work towards is a great way to shut out societal slutshaming and focus on what you genuinely want from sex. There is bravery in choosing to have the sex you've been desiring, whether that's having sex for the first time, having a threesome or trying a new sex act you've been curious about. The more we embrace the sex life we want to have, the easier it becomes to see the value of sex, and how ridiculous slutshaming really is.

If you know wholeheartedly that you are consciously having sex that follows your values and brings you joy, then you'll be able to laugh in the face of slutshaming.

Having unapologetic, pleasurable sex – and figuring out what that looks like for you – also teaches you so much about your mind and body and how they work together. This is a revolutionary act in a world of slutshaming.

Pleasure is a lot more important than we give it credit for. In fact, the World Health Organization considers sex to be part of our overall quality of life, as important as social activity, sleep quality, our home environment and our feelings.

Pleasure is about that moment when you're in the bedroom, alone or with a partner, and something happens that sparks a reaction in you. It's that feeling of joy, mixed with satisfaction and intimacy.

The true consequences of slutshaming

That is pleasure. When you think about how amazing that feels, it makes no sense at all to shame it, does it?

I believe sexual pleasure is a human right. If it's been taken from you by societal structures, you have every reason to fight against that and take back what's yours. It's up to us now.

Slutshaming in healthcare

Did you *also* know that women who are perceived as sluts are less likely to receive the support they need from healthcare professionals? In the research study 'Dehumanization in Medicine: Causes, Solutions, and Functions', it was discovered that healthcare workers in Australia have less empathy for women they perceive to be sluts. And we also know that people have biases and preconceived ideas about who is or isn't a slut, based on things like their race or class.

A UC San Diego study explored patient reactions to guilt and shame in its research 'When a Doctor's Visit Is a Guilt Trip' and found that twenty-six per cent of women were shamed by a physician, compared to fifteen per cent of the men surveyed. Both men and women were most likely to be shamed for their sex lives, especially for casual sex, as well as for their weight.

Twenty-nine-year-old Rebekah from New York, USA, tells me she was slutshamed by her doctor when she shared her concerns that she had an STI. Her doctor asked her if the person she was having sex with was her boyfriend, and when she said no, he told her a committed relationship was the best way to avoid STIs. Twenty-one-year-old Lily* from Sheffield, UK, experienced a very similar conversation, as did thirty-three-year-old Natalie* from Australia. Not one of them received the truest and most helpful advice, which is that practising safe sex with condoms is, of course, the best way to prevent STIs.

The outcome of this medical slutshaming can be very dangerous. People need to be able to have open conversations with medical professionals about sex for a variety of reasons. For instance, questions about someone's sex life can lead to diagnoses for a range of illnesses, from cancer to mental health conditions. Unexpected changes in sexual activity, or struggles in the bedroom, such as sexual dysfunction, can sometimes (but not always) point to a larger health issue, so doctors need to have all those details.

Many patients find sharing this kind of information very difficult. So if a doctor responds with judgement or slutshaming or a lack of empathy, patients are less likely to divulge important details, which can mean important diagnoses are missed.

Everyone deserves to be listened to and empathized with by their doctor, regardless of their sexual history.

Advocating for yourself

If you notice or suspect your doctor is showing any sort of bias, you have a right to speak up. I know this can be difficult – for some people more than others – but your advocacy may lead to better support for you and future patients.

There are a few things you can say to a healthcare provider if you believe they are slutshaming or discriminating against you in any way.

- It's important for me to be able to share my sexual history so I can be diagnosed and treated effectively. Can you leave your personal opinions outside of this room?
- I don't think my sexual history is relevant here. Can you explain why you are asking me this question?
- I don't think your opinions on my lifestyle should affect your ability to treat me.
- I've read that people tend to get less empathy and access to medical support if they're perceived as promiscuous, and I just want to make sure that's not happening here.
- Can I speak to another doctor about this?
- I feel you are not taking my concerns seriously.
- Can you make a note in my record that I requested this test and you denied it?

If you're having trouble with a medical provider, it's also OK to raise a formal complaint by visiting their website and filing an

241

official complaint. Or you can ask at reception to speak to the director of the practice. Another option is to search for an alternative provider. You are the owner of your body, and you are always the one in charge. You're allowed to ask for things to be handled differently, and you can feed back when things do not feel right. You have the right to create the changes you need, to make yourself more comfortable.

We all deserve abortion access

Sexual behaviour, and the morality surrounding it, worms its way into conversations about abortion all the time.

As I'm writing, it's a difficult time for people needing an abortion in certain countries. *Roe v. Wade* – the USA's landmark Supreme Court decision that officially ruled abortion to be a constitutional right – was overturned in 2022. As a result, individual states were granted the power to decide on abortion rights. Within six months of losing *Roe v. Wade*, twenty-four states had banned abortion in some capacity. Some banned it outright, while others only allowed abortion in specific circumstances, such as rape and incest.

In mainland Europe, ninety-five per cent of women of reproductive age live in countries that do allow abortion; the UK and Ireland have patchy and confused laws surrounding abortion access. In some areas, including England and Wales, abortion is still technically criminalized but largely accessible, meaning women can usually get

The true consequences of slutshaming

abortions but they are not legally protected. In other words, if you want to have an abortion, you can, but there's technically nothing stopping you from being prosecuted for it.

For instance, in 2023, a woman in England was prosecuted and charged with prison time for having an abortion late into her pregnancy, based on the Offences Against the Person Act, which was enacted in 1861 and hasn't been updated with regard to abortion since. As for Ireland, abortion was decriminalized in 2019, but there still are not enough providers in the country for us to truly be able to say, confidently, that all women have access to abortion there.

Abortions are thankfully also legal in Australia, New Zealand and Japan, within a certain time frame. They are available for anyone who needs an abortion and not just in particular circumstances, such as if they are a victim of rape.

While of course it is important to consider rape victims in the abortion debate, only allowing abortions for rape victims perpetuates the idea that a woman needs to be violated in order to be granted bodily autonomy. It makes it clear that anyone asking for an abortion because they've simply been enjoying sex and an unwanted pregnancy has occurred doesn't deserve to have one.

'What about the rape victims?' seems to be the go-to argument, and I know it can feel like a helpful question in the abortion debate, but actually it speaks to how ingrained purity culture is.

Whether we like it or not, we gravitate to the purest examples of 'perfect victims' (a messed-up concept we'll explore later) when fighting against injustice and screw ourselves over in the process. It sends the message that unwanted pregnancies are punishments for promiscuity. (Remind me again why they want us to raise children with that mindset?)

It's not helpful to ignore the women who have chosen to have sex and fallen pregnant. Especially as, according to the Centers for Disease Control and Prevention, more unwanted pregnancies come from consensual sex where contraception isn't used (or is used incorrectly) than out of violence.

It goes without saying that women who have been raped deserve an abortion if they want to have one. But so do the women who love casual sex with multiple partners. So do the women who have just one partner. Absolutely everyone deserves this right. It's paramount that we keep this in mind whenever we discuss abortion. While well-meaning and understandable, the 'what if she was raped?' question that always comes up in abortion discourse is unhelpful.

Sluts don't deserve justice

Slutshaming not only restricts our access to healthcare, but also significantly impacts the way that the justice system works. This is the case for most crimes – even women who are on trial for murder are publicly slutshamed, as though it's linked to their crime. But

The true consequences of slutshaming

the crime most drastically impacted by slutshaming is rape and sexual assault.

The first time I sent an intimate picture to my boyfriend as a teenager, it was just for fun. We thought we were in love, and I wanted to send him sexy images and videos of myself. As the camera flashed and I contorted my body in various positions, draped in my favourite underwear, I never imagined the pictures being captured would be used to paint a very particular picture of me years later – one that would not only shame me, but justify harm done to me.

I started going out with this boyfriend a long time ago and I thought we had a cute, almost enviable relationship. I showed him off, and I liked doing that. I bragged to other girls about our sex life, and sending sexts and exchanging nudes was a big part of that.

But when you're not looking for red flags, obsession can easily be mistaken for love. He would wait for me outside everywhere I went – even to my workplace , where he'd hang around, watching me. I was eventually fired for letting my boyfriend 'come in and distract me' and as I started to think about my future and what I wanted it to look like, he tried to control that too.

You may notice that I'm being incredibly vague about our relationship, who he was to me and who I was at the time, and that's entirely on purpose. Jess Phillipps, MP of Birmingham Yardley in the UK, is one of many outspoken feminists to point out the ways that women who endure abuse are silenced and even attacked through defamation lawsuits. In an article in the *Guardian*, she says, 'There was "a worrying trend" where, after #MeToo and women being encouraged to take to social media to accuse their alleged abusers, they were subsequently having to deal with the ramifications of publishing their experiences.'

I don't wish to be one of the many women who are bullied into submission and silence with legal threats, so until the justice system improves – which we will get to – I'm choosing to not mention the details of my relationship. I'd love to tell you everything, to show that I'm not afraid of him (because I'm truly not), and that if you've gone through something similar, you're not alone. I hope that I can do that anyway, while protecting my safety in our messed up legal world.

The next months of my life with this boyfriend were some of the worst, when it should have been an exciting time of putting plans in motion for starting my career. Abusive boys and men are way smarter than we give them credit for. He was calculated in the way he implanted guilt in me, emotionally abusing me and telling me I was responsible for his poor mental health.

Some days he actively tried to convince me that I was a horrible girlfriend for considering moving away from him when I knew he couldn't live without me. Other days he pressured me into looking at private flats instead of shared accommodation so that he could come with me.

The true consequences of slutshaming

Gaslighting is a form of domestic abuse where a partner tries to make you believe you are crazy or mistaken when you know, logically, that you are not. They might tell you that you were too drunk to remember anything properly when you bring up something you were unhappy about from the night before – even when you weren't that drunk. Or they might tell you that your feelings are not valid because you're a 'sensitive' or 'dramatic' person.

Within a month of the gaslighting starting, my boyfriend began sexually assaulting me. Before long, he was raping me whenever we saw each other. Some days he coerced me with manipulative words about his despair and feelings of suicide. Other days he didn't say anything and used physical force instead.

It's hard to describe the heaviness of being betrayed in this way by someone you love, and by someone who was supposed to love you too. I grew up believing rapists were creepy men hiding in alleyways and lurking outside night clubs, not the boy you can't imagine being gone from your life, who you have been dating and who lies in bed next to you.

I escaped the relationship after finally telling my mum what he had been doing to me. She helped me break up with him – a deed done over the phone to avoid further violence and a swift hang-up before he could shout at me – and dedicated her time to helping me recover.

I tried to move on by focusing on college and my new part-time supermarket job, but my mental health was rapidly deteriorating. I suffered horribly from insomnia, flashbacks, disassociation, anxiety and intrusive thoughts. I damaged almost every friendship I had with my new-found insecurities, paranoia and lack of self-esteem.

Unable to recognize myself any more, I decided to report him to the police. I knew that I deserved justice, but I'd avoided reporting him up until that point because I didn't want him to get hurt. But now I knew this had to happen, so I could be free.

They arrested him swiftly after my exhausting six-hour initial interview, in which I had to describe the near-decade we'd known one another. After being literally assaulted, I felt like I was being re-assaulted with questions such as, 'What were you wearing?', 'How would you describe your sex drive?' and 'What about his sex drive?' Then they took our devices to evidence labs so they could collect messages and images we'd exchanged.

After a year-long battle, with cold and inconsistent communication from the Crown Prosecution Service (CPS), my case was abruptly dismissed because of the sexual messages and imagery my ex and I had exchanged, along with texts revealing I'd been unfaithful (I had kissed someone at a house party during a brief break we had both agreed to).

The true consequences of slutshaming

The anger in my ex's messages pointed to infidelity, according to the CPS, and they said that this could be seen as the reason for our break-up rather than the abuse I'd outlined in my statement.

'You will be ripped to shreds in court,' the CPS investigator told me. 'You didn't mention the images or the cheating before, so it looks bad now. Especially the images. They'll use it to discredit you.'

It didn't matter that the sexting had occurred before my ex-boyfriend's abusive behaviour began, or that the cheating happened during it. My case was now cold.

The same study which I refer to earlier in the book – whose finding saw that seventy-nine per cent of people will be slutshamed at some point during their lifetime – also says that most of those slutshaming victims will also experience sexual harassment at a higher rate.

In fact, the two go hand in hand. Slutshaming puts a target on women's backs. To be called a slut or shamed for sexual expression lets the wider community know that this person is to be treated badly, and that it's OK to treat them badly.

It tells them that, as a slut, they can be ridiculed, humiliated, ignored, denied access to certain resources, communities or opportunities, and in the worst cases subjected to harm.

I lost my rape case because of sexual images I'd sent during the brief happy part of my relationship and because I'd had sexual contact with someone else behind my boyfriend's back. The message was loud and clear – I didn't deserve justice because I was a slut.

I'm not alone in my experience. My case didn't even make it to trial because of my perceived slutty behaviour. In an article for *British Glamour*, Lucy Morgan explores the deeply ingrained beliefs about sluts that can sway cases in favour of the perpetrator.

Rape convictions are at an all-time low in the UK. In England and Wales, more than ninety-nine per cent of rapes reported to police do not end in a conviction, despite the number of sexual offences logged reaching a record high of 193,566 in 2023, according to figures obtained by the Labour Party. It was also found that nearly seventy per cent of rape survivors dropped out of the justice system in the fourth quarter of 2022. Considering that slutshaming is practically an official investigation technique when it comes to rape cases, it doesn't surprise me. I wish I had dropped out too.

As for the USA, only 0.7 per cent of cases for rapes and attempted rapes end with a felony conviction for the perpetrator.

In Australia, just 1.5 per cent of cases result in a conviction. The cases can be brutal and lengthy, and it's no surprise that, with so

The true consequences of slutshaming

many perpetrators walking free, eighty-seven per cent of sexual assault cases go unreported in Australia.

In the UK, those accused of rape and sexual assault are tried by a jury, meaning the evidence for their alleged crimes is examined by a group of ordinary members of the public (twelve people if you're in England, Wales and Northern Ireland; fifteen in Scotland), who ultimately determine whether you are found innocent, guilty or sometimes, as in Scotland, 'not proven'.

The Scottish government is currently debating whether the jury should be removed from rape and sexual assault trials, to see if this helps trials become more effective at prosecuting rape cases.

Jurors have been found to overassess the sex lives, sexual history, clothing and appearance of rape victims. This is why feminist campaigners and legal professionals support the idea of rape trials without a jury. Morgan writes how they are 'too often swayed by rape myths', such as:

- Rape victims aren't deserving of sympathy if they were drunk at the time
- Rape victims are 'asking for it' if they wear slutty clothing
- Rape victims' previous consensual sexual behaviour is proof of whether or not a person has been raped
- Rape victims are more likely to lie about rape if they've slept with a lot of people before

These commonly believed myths can influence the jury's verdicts in many cases. Basically, if a rape victim is seen as a slut, like I was, they're less likely to receive justice.

This can be seen in an infamous rape case from 2018 in Ireland, wherein a twenty-seven-year-old man was accused of raping a seventeen-year-old woman in an alleyway. During the closing argument for the trial, the defence lawyer asked the jury to consider the underwear worn by the victim at the time. 'Does the evidence out-rule the possibility that she was attracted to the defendant and was open to meeting someone and being with someone?' the lawyer asked, according to the *Irish Times*.

'You have to look at the way she was dressed. She was wearing a thong with a lace front,' he added.

The man accused of raping her was not charged with any crime, and the victim did not receive any justice.

The case immediately sparked a national dialogue about consent, slutshaming and victim-blaming. Hundreds of women and men with posters and lace underwear in hand protested in five cities across the country the following day.

Though my case was dropped in 2015, and the case in Ireland took place in 2019, very little has changed.

The true consequences of slutshaming

Lucia Osborne-Crowley, a legal reporter and the author of *My Body Keeps Your Secrets*, tells me that slutshaming is still frequently used by defence lawyers as a method for discrediting victims in courtrooms in the UK and Ireland. She notes that it's also a common tactic in the USA. However, it's under-reported in a lot of other countries.

She talks about the digital download law, which is a law that allows police to take a victim's phone and download everything on it to be considered as evidence (as I experienced in my own case). The UK is one of the only jurisdictions in the world that does this.

To put it plainly, this law should not exist. The digital download law is used to look for very specific criteria in victims' camera rolls and messages. 'Slutshaming is a major part of that strategy. They look for consensual sexual messaging between the victim and the perpetrator,' Osborne-Crowley adds, which, as we know, should have no bearing on a rape case.

'Even if there's concrete evidence of rape in a case, previous sexual history, even if it's not with the perpetrator, can throw a case out.'

It would actually be easy to prevent slutshaming in investigations, and subsequently in courtrooms, in many countries. Osborne-Crowly explains how we already have a clear legal definition of consent on our side in the UK, for instance. So to stop the slutshaming in the justice system, you wouldn't even need to pass new legislation. It would simply mean banning defence lawyers from asking anything about *consensual* sex or nude-sharing.

She says, 'That kind of thing should not come anywhere near a rape charge or any kind of sexual violence charge. If it's consensual, it has nothing to do with the crime.'

The perfect victim

Unfortunately, we aren't there yet, though. And these slutshaming myths leave rape victims feeling like they must come across as the 'perfect victim'. In practice, this essentially means wearing modest clothing to not look promiscuous, to increase their chances of being believed.

Abuse specialist Evie Muir explains how most of us conjure a very specific image of what a woman who is telling the truth about being assaulted looks like. She's probably white, able-bodied, cisgender, straight and conservative. And she's definitely not a slut.

As we know, there is a disproportionate risk of sexual violence against working-class women, women of colour and queer people. Part of challenging slutshaming is challenging our perceptions about what victims of violence look like. Victims can be working-class, people of colour, disabled people, fat people, thin people, transgender people, sluts. Literally anyone can be a victim of sexual assault. It doesn't discriminate.

Think about it: we know that one in three women globally are raped. Would it be possible for all of those women to look like the picture of privilege?

Making real change

It's easy to read all these stories and stats and feel like the world is impossibly bleak. Researching rape culture, and living through it, has often filled me with such a heavy sadness that I've felt uncharacteristically hopeless at times.

But what helps me feel positive again is seeing the powerful campaigning from individuals and grassroots organizations that has not only shown the good in the world but has, at times, created significant change.

Swedish laws

Women's rights campaigners put a lot of pressure on the Swedish government to change the legal definition of rape to 'sex without consent'. The previous definition of rape only included the horror-movie kind of rape that happens violently, by a stranger. This meant that prosecutors had to show evidence of the use of threat, physical violence or coercion to prove a rape case. Unfortunately, women are most likely to be sexually assaulted by someone they know, so these kinds of definitions are unhelpful and dangerous.

Thankfully, they made the change in 2018. And in the two years that followed, rape conviction rates saw a seventy-five per cent rise. Women's rights campaigners are now calling on other countries to follow Sweden's example. Germany's rape convictions also rose by forty-eight per cent after their laws were updated to have more specific definitions of consent and following those definitions in the courtroom.

Changing the courtrooms

There are also a range of court reporters, such as Lucia Osborne-Crowley, and judges, for example Dr Charlotte Proudman, who have made a conscious effort to educate themselves on misogyny in courtrooms. They have researched slutshaming and how preconceived ideas and biases around sluts can play a role in convictions. They have dedicated their careers to highlighting cases where this happens and are working hard to change it.

Speaking in schools

Along with changes in the courtroom, there are incredible people striving to pull rape culture out of society by the roots. Gina Martin, activist and author of *"No Offence, But . . .": How to Have Difficult Conversations for Meaningful Change*, is best known for making upskirting illegal (i.e. taking non-consensual sexual photographs of someone). She wrote in the *Guardian* in 2023 that she is now training to run workshops for young boys about gender, shame, equality and sex. This way, Martin believes, she will be able to change rape culture by preventing rape, rather than focusing on punishments for rape after it happens.

'This is why I speak in schools across the UK, as well as raise funds for grassroots organisations. There may not be a big, sparkly win, but there will be consistent impact in the form of smaller wins,' she writes.

This is also something that comes up in the work of Andrew Hampton, a former headteacher, education expert and author of *Working with Boys: Creating Cultures of Mutual Respect in Schools.*

Hampton believes that reducing sexual assault and rape comes down to teaching young boys about shame and humiliation, encouraging them to embrace and normalize those feelings rather than retaliate against them. He is committed to overhauling lessons about consent in schools to include this important subject.

Artistic activism

Art can also play a part in challenging rape myths. According to The Center for Artistic Activism, creating art to challenge political or social norms is an effective non-violent approach that has the power to create 'moving experiences that prompt people to question the world in its current state'.

Anti-slutshaming art thrives online, particularly on Instagram, in accounts such as Slut Social, Cliterally the Best, Venus Libido, AOTEAROTICA, Jacq Moon and more.

The touring 'What Were You Wearing?' exhibit which debuted at the University of Kansas in 2014 is a perfect example of art creating action. The exhibit presented eighteen accounts of sexual assault, together with images of the clothing each victim wore at the time of their attack. The exhibition is designed to confront how often women are vilified for their clothing and told they need to 'cover up' to prevent being raped. A swimsuit, a small child's yellow-collared shirt, a sexy red dress, and a T-shirt and trousers are among the outfits featured.

The project was launched in 2013 by Dr Mary A. Wyandt-Hiebert, who directs all programming initiatives at the University of Arkansas' rape education centre, and Jen Brockman, director of KU's Sexual Assault Prevention and Education Center. Following its creation and debut in 2014, the installation has been on display at a number of different universities across the USA.

Since it was first displayed, the exhibit has attracted global press coverage and sparked much-needed conversations about slutshaming and rape culture.

The true consequences of slutshaming

Chinese artist Yawen Deng also created a series of photographs taking apart slutshaming in Chinese culture, centred around the only female emperor in Chinese history, Wu Zetian, placing her in 'feminine clothing to create an anti-traditional "slut" image'.

With so many inspiring people and organizations demanding and creating change like this, I will always remain hopeful that slutshaming can be removed from healthcare systems, courtrooms and across the many parts of society through which it currently runs.

Angry?

I am too. And we are perfectly justified in being angry about everything we've discussed. I also wouldn't blame you if you feel sad or bogged down. When faced with the facts of how far slutshaming can truly go, it's easy to feel like it's won already. But it hasn't.

Your safety is not a privilege. It's a human right.

Slutshaming is a construct, and you are a real person with value who deserves to have the sex you want without fear. That's a future we can genuinely work towards. We have more control over rape culture and healthcare restrictions than you might think. History has proved that day-to-day people like me and you can create significant, important change if we're defiant and work together.

That's why I wrote this book – because I felt sad and alone and I wanted to do something about the horrors of slutshaming. I wanted to spread the word, and I wanted *Sluts* to be a rallying cry to get more people to help.

The sadness and fear that comes with facing how we've gone wrong as a society isn't always something to back away from. Instead, let's use it to push us forward and end slutshaming.

Conclusion
The power of the slut

I love being a slut. I hope that after reading this book you love being a slut too. Maybe you're not ready to use the word, and maybe you'll never be comfortable with it, and that's OK. But I hope this book *has* helped you feel ready to embark on your journey to fight slutshaming.

I know it can be really difficult to stay sex positive in such a sex negative world. You're constantly battling with slutshaming messages. And these messages come from everywhere – from people you know, the media and the systems that underpin our society. Sometimes it can be hard to block out that noise. I get it.

I live my life in a very slutty way. My house is overflowing with sex toys, which has provoked plenty of weird comments from builders and plumbers and the various other people my landlord sends over to fix things. I write about sex for a living and talk about sex all the time. I just wrote a whole book about sex.

And yet even I still get tripped up by the odd slutshaming 'hot take' I see online every now and then. Just recently, a tweet ground my morning scrolling to a halt as it was claiming women aren't 'real classy women' any more because they have such high body counts. In the same week, the agony aunt of a popular British newspaper told a worried husband who had written in about how he was intimidated by his wife's sexual history that the wife had been cruel and should have kept that information to herself. Sometimes, you can feel surrounded by slutshaming, and it can just make you want to conform and spare yourself the consequences of being different.

You might find that, as you choose to embark on your anti-slutshaming journey, you get tripped up like this sometimes too. We're trying to change the way society works here, and that isn't an easy feat. You might find slutshaming ideas sneaking into your sex life next time you're trying out something new in the bedroom. You might spot yourself judging someone for their body count, or spending a little too much time fixating on your own number of sexual partners. You might make a quick assumption about someone because of the way they are dressed.

The power of the slut

You are only human, and none of this is your fault. We are going up against multiple powerful systems in our fight against slutshaming and you're going to make some mistakes.

You are brave and incredible and powerful just for aiming to be sex positive in this climate.

It's important to remember that these systems we are trying to unravel are not the truth. They are just systems. Someone put them in place, and therefore we can kick them back out again. We don't have to live by them, even if it sometimes seems like everyone else is.

Whether you accidentally find yourself slutshaming someone or you experience slutshaming yourself, or you see it happening from afar, I want you to channel your feelings into action.

You know now what slutshaming looks like, the purity culture it stems from and the double standards around it. You know just how much damage slutshaming can do, and you know how it can impact different people, particularly those marginalized sections of the population. You know that challenging all those systems, including capitalism, racism and homophobia, are all part of fighting sexism.

You know that there are incredible people all over the world working hard to dismantle the systems that keep slutshaming alive. You know that there are grassroots campaigns, organizations, charities and individuals fighting slutshaming in schools, spreading awareness about rape culture, improving sex education and campaigning for marginalized groups. You know that you can join them in myriad ways and fight slutshaming with whatever you have to give.

You also now have your own sexual trajectory – a path that aligns with your values. And I can't wait for your journey to begin.

After I was sexually assaulted (and after a ton of therapy), having the sex I wanted felt like a form of justice when I couldn't get that in the courtroom: an opportunity to reclaim my sexuality and figure out who I was.

It was through casual sex that I learned how to have sex, what I liked and how to get the pleasure that I needed and deserved.

Sex, even in abundance, is no bad thing. You are not greedy or dirty or bad for loving it.

But to me, being a slut isn't only about casual sex. It's about being unafraid to figure out what brings you joy, and to go after it unapologetically. That might look like sleeping around, it might look like having sex within a committed relationship, or it might look like sticking on some fluffy socks, lighting a candle and having a wank. Whatever works best for you is your choice and no one else's.

Whatever sex you're having, as long as it's done safely, is no one else's business. We all deserve pleasure and we should prioritize it unapologetically.

Sluts are so often portrayed as broken, but when you're slutshamed by others it's because they're afraid you'll be the one doing the breaking. Our sexual freedom poses a threat to the systems that we are trying to fight against.

And in a world where you can be anything, be a threat.

Where to look for more information

Books have word counts (for good reason) and while we were extensive in our learnings here, there's only ever going to be so much information provided in one book. If this is the first book you've ever picked up about slutshaming, I advise you to keep going. The more information we have, the better we are armed against patriarchy and its sexual control. Here is additional reading for if you would like to delve further into the subject.

For more information about whorephobia, read *Whorephobia: Strippers on Art, Work, and Life* by Lizzie Borden (Seven Stories Press 2022)

For more about the myth of the sex drive, read *Mind the Gap: The Truth About Desire and How to Futureproof Your Sex Life* by Dr Karen Gurney (Headline Home 2020)

267

Find more on purity culture in general in *The Purity Myth* by Jessica Valenti (Seal Press, 2009)

To read more about classism, read *Chavs: the Demonization of the Working Class* by Owen Jones (Verso Books, 2011)

For more about how our language and actions around oppressive systems can be counter-productive, and what to do instead, read *"No Offence, But . . .": How to Have Difficult Conversations for Meaningful Change* by Gina Martin (Bantam, 2023)

Find more information about racism in *Why I'm No Longer Talking to White People About Race* by Reni Eddo-Lodge (Bloomsbury Circus, 2017)

For more on bisexuality and slutshaming, read *Boyslut: A Memoir and Manifesto* by Zachary Zane (Abrams Image, 2023)

Read more about Section 28's impact on sex education and queer culture in *Outrageous!: The Story of Section 28 and Britain's Battle for LGBT Education* by Paul Baker (Reaktion Books, 2022)

For an exploration of transgender lives and analysis of how transgender people are vilified in society, read *The Transgender Issue: A Case for Justice* by Shon Faye (Allen Lane, 2021)

Where to look for more information

For more on sexual double standards in slutshaming, read 'He is a Stud, She is a Slut! A Meta-Analysis on the Continued Existence of Sexual Double Standards', *Personality and Social Psychology Review*, 24(2):163–190, by Joyce J. Endendijk, Anneloes L. van Baar and Maja Deković (2019)

To read about sex positivity's origins in witchcraft, read *Witches, Sluts, Feminists: Conjuring the Sex Positive* by Kristen J. Sollee (ThreeL Media, 2017)

A deep dive into witch trials and why they still impact women today can be found in *In Defence of Witches: Why women are still on trial* by Mona Chollet (Picador, 2023)

For more about having the sex you want, and not the sex everyone else wants you to have, read *Come as You Are: the surprising new science that will transform your sex life* by Emily Nagoski (Scribe UK, 2015)

For information on how sex myths can affect our relationships and our desire function, read 'The Relationship between Sexual Functioning and Sexual Concordance in Women', in *Journal of Sex & Marital Therapy*, by K. D. Suschinsky, J. S. Huberman, L. Maunder, L. A. Brotto, T. Hollenstein and M. L. Chivers (2019)

For information on how the Madonna-whore complex and slutshaming applies to plus size women, read 'The Madonna-Whore-Victim Complex: Fat Girl and Piggy' in Polyester Zine online

And for more information on how BDSM- and kink-shaming interlinks with slutshaming, read 'It's time to talk more about kink – and take the shame away from it' in the *Guardian*, by R. O. Kwon (9 February 2021)

References

Introduction

Tanenbaum, Leora, *Slut!: Growing Up Female with a Bad Reputation*, Harper Perennial, 2000

Goblet, Margot & Glowacz, Fabienne, 'Slut Shaming in Adolescence: A Violence Against Girls and Its Impact on their Health', *International Journal of Environmental Research and Public Health*, 18(12):6657, 21 June 2021, www.ncbi.nlm.nih.gov/pmc/articles/PMC8296320/

Tanenbaum, Leora, 'The Truth About Slut-Shaming', Huffpost.com, 15 April 2015, www.huffpost.com/entry/the-truth-about-slut-shaming_b_7054162

Chapter One: What is slutshaming?

Laderer, Ashley, 'Women Share Slut Shaming Stories – and Admit Why They Do it Themselves', *Teen Vogue*, 27 November 2017, www.teenvogue.com/story/women-share-slut-shaming-stories-and-admit-why-they-do-it-themselves

Resnick, Ariane, 'What Is Slut-Shaming?', 7 June 2023, www.verywellmind.com/what-is-slut-shaming-5271893

Gordon, Sherri, 'What Is Slut-Shaming?', 2 September 2022, www.verywellfamily.com/the-effects-of-slut-shaming-on-teen-girls-460586

Khazan, Olga, 'There's No Such Thing as a Slut', *The Atlantic*, 28 May 2014, www.theatlantic.com/health/archive/2014/05/theres-no-such-thing-as-a-slut/371773/

Catherine Hill, Ph.D., and Holly Kearl, M.A, 'Crossing the Line: Sexual Harassment at School', 2011, https://www.aauw.org/resources/research/crossing-the-line-sexual-harassment-at-school/

Grace, Asia, 'Teens slam school's "sexist" dress code: "It perpetuates rape culture"', *New York Post*, 9 June 2021, nypost.com/2021/06/09/teens-bare-bellies-to-protest-schools-sexist-dress-code/

Hobman, Jade, 'Aussie students are being sent to detention because their short skirts are "distracting" male staff and students – as furious schoolgirls fire back over the "sexist" rules', MailOnline, 3 June 2022, www.dailymail.co.uk/news/article-10881163/Melbourne-schoolgirls-call-sexism-teachers-detention-short-skirts.html

References

Carroll, Rory, 'Students protest "slut shaming" high school dress codes with mass walkouts', *Guardian*, 24 September 2014, www.theguardian.com/education/2014/sep/24/us-high-schools-dress-codes-protest-sexism-hemline

Venn, Lydia, 'Uni is meant to be about sexual freedom so why are girls still being slut shamed?' *The Tab,* 2022, thetab.com/uk/2022/02/21/uni-is-meant-to-be-about-sexual-freedom-so-why-are-girls-still-being-slut-shamed-241490

Martin, Gina, *"No Offence, But . . .": How to Have Difficult Conversations for Meaningful Change*, Bantam, 2023

Hess, Wendy, 'Slut-Shaming in the Workplace: Sexual Rumors & Hostile Claims', *New York University Review of Law & Social Change*, 40(581), 2016, papers.ssrn.com/sol3/papers.cfm?abstract_id=3461414

Oppenheim, Maya, 'Daily Mail accused of 'appalling sexism' for comparing Theresa May and Nicola Sturgeon's legs on front page', *The Independent,* 29 Mar 2017

Childnet International, 'Young people's experiences of online sexual harassment: A cross-country report from Project deSHAME', 2017

ABC News Australia, 'Senator Eric Abetz accused of "slut-shaming" Brittany Higgins', www.youtube.com/watch?v=gofxhIxcjM8

https://www.abc.net.au/news/2021-03-24/mp-accuses-senator-eric-abetz-of-slut-shaming-brittany-higgins/100016180

Murphy, Katherine, 28 November 2018, *Guardian,* "Why parliament still tolerates thuggery not acceptable in broader society" https://www.theguardian.com/australia-news/2018/nov/28/why-parliament-still-tolerates-thuggery-not-acceptable-in-broader-society

Chapter Two: You don't owe anyone purity

Klein, Linda Kay, *Pure: Inside the Evangelical Movement that Shamed a Generation of Young Women and How I Broke Free,* Atria Books, 2018

Klein, Linda Kay, 'What is purity culture?', lindakayklein.com/what-is-purity-culture/

Munger, Kelsey L., 'Purity culture slut-shame blues: Everything I know about sex I learned from Bob Dylan', 23 October 2016, www.salon.com/2016/10/23/purity-culture-slut-shame-blues-everything-i-know-about-sex-i-learned-from-bob-dylan/

Engle, Gigi, *All the F*cking Mistakes: A Guide to Sex, Love, and Life,* St Martin's Griffin, 2020

Huang, Howard, 'Cherry Picking: Virginity Loss Definitions Among Gay and Straight Cisgender Men', Taylor Francis Online,

References

2017, www.tandfonline.com/doi/full/10.1080/00918369.2017.1364110

Schechter, Florence, *V: An empowering celebration of the vulva and vagina*, Penguin, 2023

Gautam, Biswas, *Review of Forensic Medicine and Toxicology*, Jaypee Brothers Medical Publishers, 2021

Smith Galer, Sophia, *Losing It: Sex Education for the 21st Century*, William Collins, 2022

Taylor, Marisa, 'Slut-shaming has little to do with sex, study finds', Aljazeera America, 29 May 2014, america.aljazeera.com/articles/2014/5/29/slut-shaming-study.html

Rosenbloom, Stephanie, 'A Ring That Says No, Not Yet', 8 December 2005, *The New York Times*, www.nytimes.com/2005/12/08/fashion/thursdaystyles/a-ring-that-says-no-not-yet.html

Green, Emma, 'Americans: Still Pretty Judge-y', *The Atlantic*, 9 June 2014, www.theatlantic.com/national/archive/2014/06/americans-still-pretty-judge-y/372414/

Anthony Paik et al, 'Broken Promises: Abstinence Pledging and Sexual and Reproductive Health', University of

Massachusetts – Amherst, 2016 *Wiley Online Library,* https://onlinelibrary.wiley.com/doi/abs/10.1111/jomf.12279.

Ott, Mary A. & Santelli, John S., 'Abstinence and abstinence-only education', *Current Opinion in Obstetrics and Gynecology,* 19(5):446-452, October 2007, www.ncbi.nlm.nih.gov/pmc/articles/PMC5913747/#:~:text=Using%20the%20nationally%20representative%20Annenberg,abstinence%2Donly%20to%20be%20effective.

Engle, Gigi, 'How growing up in purity culture impact sex', *Mashable,* 3 August 2023, mashable.com/article/purity-culture-impact-sex

Tempera, Jacqueline, 'What It Means To Have A Soul Tie—And How To Break An Unhealthy Connection', *Women's Health,* 3 September 2023

Green, Sarah, 'I Grew Up In A Hyper-Evangelical Church In Britain. Here's Why I Left', *Refinery29,* 18 April 2022, www.refinery29.com/en-gb/2022/04/10934517/purity-culture-christianity-britain

Hong, Angie, 'The Flaw at the Center of Purity Culture', *The Atlantic,* 28 March 2021, www.theatlantic.com/ideas/archive/2021/03/purity-culture-evangelical-church-harms-women/618438/

References

Sex Education Forum 'Young People's Relationships and Sex Education Poll 2022', 2 March 2023, https://www.sexeducation forum.org.uk/resources/evidence/young-peoples-rse-poll-2022

Lee, Chris, 'What's wrong with sex education in Japan?', *Zenbird*, 5 April 2020 zenbird.media/whats-wrong-with-sex-education-in-japan/

Sijapati, Aasna, 'The Troubling Lack of Sexual Education In South Asia', *The* Gazelle, 10 November 2018, www.thegazelle.org/ issue/145/the-troubling-lack-of-sexual-education-in-south-asia

Badarudin Badarudin & Andriani, Ana, 'Sexual Issues and Prevention Through Sex Education in Primary School', *Atlantis Press*, November 2016 https://www.atlantis-press.com/proceedings/ icece-16/25869300

European Commission, 2023, "Sexuality education across the European Union: an overview"

Act for Kids, Australia It's Time To Get Comfy with Sex Ed, August 2022, https://www.actforkids.com.au/

Sex and HIV Education, 1 September 2023, Guttmacher Institute https://www.guttmacher.org/state-policy/explore/sex-and-hiv-education

Glenza, Jessica, 'America's abstinence-only sex ed: what is taught in public schools?', *Guardian*, 25 August 2015 https://www.theguardian.com/us-news/2015/aug/25/abstinence-only-sex-education-public-schools-quiz

Choosing the Best PATH, www.choosingthebest.com/path

Erens, B., 'National survey of sexual attitudes and lifestyles (2003)', London School of Hygiene & Tropical Medicine, core.ac.uk/download/pdf/42631008.pdf

Q&A, 'Comprehensive sexuality education', World Health Organization, 18 May 2023, www.who.int/news-room/questions-and-answers/item/comprehensive-sexuality-education

Riffkin, Rebecca, 'New Record Highs in Moral Acceptability', 30 May 2014, *Gallup*, news.gallup.com/poll/170789/new-record-highs-moral-acceptability.aspx

Chapter Three: The true history of sluts

Sleigh, Jon, ' "Intolerably bent on carnality" – The Life and Death of Lady Frances Carr', Whores of Yore, 11 March 2019, www.thewhoresofyore.com/sex-history/intolerably-bent-on-carnality-the-life-and-death-of-lady-frances-carr-by-jon-sleigh

References

Clark, Meredith, 'From strokes to heart attacks: Doctor highlights most commonly misdiagnosed health conditions in women', the *Independent*, 31 October 2023, https://www.independent.co.uk/life-style/health-and-families/misdiagnosed-conditions-symptoms-women-b2436662.html

Tiven, Lucy, 'The History of Slut-Shaming in One Insane Timeline, From Ancient Rome to Amber Rose', *attn:*, 1 June 2016, archive.attn.com/stories/8671/slut-shaming-history-chart

James, E. L., *Fifty Shades of Grey*, Arrow, 2012

Shakespeare, William, *As You Like It*, Act III, Scene 3, www.opensourceshakespeare.org/views/plays/play_view.php?WorkID=asyoulikeit&Act=3&Scene=3&Scope=scene

Shakespeare, William, *Much Ado About Nothing*, Act IV, Scene 1, from First Folio, 1623

Kramer, Kyra Cornelius, *The Jezebel Effect: Why the Slut Shaming of Famous Queens Still Matters*, CreateSpace Independent Publishing Platform, 2015

Sollee, Kristen J., *Witches, Sluts, Feminists: Conjuring the Sex Positive*, ThreeL Media, 2017

Brooks, Libby, 'Nicola Sturgeon issues apology for "historical injustice" of witch hunts', *Guardian*, 8 March 2022, www.theguardian.com/uk-news/2022/mar/08/nicola-sturgeon-issues-apology-for-historical-injustice-of-witch-hunts

Cramer, Maria, 'Scotland Apologizes for History of Witchcraft Persecution', *The New York Times*, 9 March 2022, www.nytimes.com/2022/03/09/world/europe/scotland-nicola-sturgeon-apologizes-witches.html

Cârstian, Maria, 'Deconstructing the "Low Other" in the First Wave of Sex Hygiene Films (1914–1919)', Stockholm University, 2019

Chapter Four: Sluts online

Kramer, Jillian, 'This is How Often a Woman Gets Called a "Slut" or a "Whore" on Twitter', *Glamour*, 31 May 2016, https://www.glamour.com/story/this-is-how-often-a-woman-gets-called-a-slut-or-a-whore-on-twitter

Geall, Lauren, & Beecham, Amy, 'Cyberflashing laws: does the Online Safety Bill go far enough to protect victims of digital sexual violence?', *Stylist*, July 2023 https://www.stylist.co.uk/news/cyberflashing-law-change/621178

Webb, Lewis, 'Shame transfigured: Slut-shaming from Rome to cyberspace', *FirstMonday*, 2015, firstmonday.org/ojs/index.php/fm/article/view/5464/4419

References

Karasavva, V., 'Putting the Y in cyberflashing: Exploring the prevalence and predictors of the reasons for sending unsolicited nude or sexual images,', *Computers in Human Behaviour Volume 140*, March 2023, https://www.sciencedirect.com/science/article/abs/pii/S0747563222004137

Lehmiller, Justin J., 'Less Sex, but More Sexual Diversity: Changes in Sexual Behavior during the COVID-19 Coronavirus Pandemic,', *Leisure Sciences Volume 43*, https://www.tandfonline.com/doi/full/10.1080/01490400.2020.1774016

Men's Health Staff, '1 In 4 Women Report Cyberflashing Has Increased During The Pandemic', *Australian Men's Health*, 3 November 2021, https://menshealth.com.au/1-in-4-women-report-cyberflashing-has-increased-during-the-pandemic/page/4/?el_dbe_page#:~:text=1%20In%204%20Women%20Report,Pandemic%20%2D%20Men's%20Health%20Magazine%20Australia

Henry, Nicola, '"Devastating, like it broke me": Responding to image-based sexual abuse in Aotearoa New Zealand', *British Society of Criminology*, 4 June 2022

Powell, Dr Anastasia & Henry, Nicola, 'One in five Australians is a victim of "revenge porn", despite new laws to prevent it', RMIT University, 23 July 2019, https://www.rmit.edu.au/news/all-news/2019/jul/revenge-porn-laws

GOV UK, 'REVENGE PORN: The Facts'

Barker, Emma, 'Cosmo Survey: 9 out of 10 Millennial Women Take Naked Photos,', *Cosmopolitan*, 3 September 2014, https://www.cosmopolitan.com/sex-love/advice/a30675/ninety-percent-millennial-women-take-nude-photos-cosmo-survey/

Burns, Janet, 'Facebook Asks Australia For Nude Pics To Test "Revenge Porn" Defense', Forbes, 7 November 2017, https://www.forbes.com/sites/janetwburns/2017/11/07/facebook-asks-for-australians-nude-pics-to-test-revenge-porn-defense/?sh=55598e667e2e

'Shocking number of people have sent nude photos, poll finds,' *New York Post*, 13 September 2022 https://nypost.com/2022/09/13/shocking-number-of-people-have-sent-nude-photos-poll-finds/

Goblet, Margot & Glowacz, Fabienne, 'Slut Shaming in Adolescence: A Violence Against Girls and Its Impact on their Health', *International Journal of Environmental Research and Public Health*, 18(12):6657, 21 June 2021, www.ncbi.nlm.nih.gov/pmc/articles/PMC8296320/

Mckinlay, Tahlee & Lavis, Tiffany, 'Why did she send it in the first place? Victim blame in the context of "revenge porn"', *Psychiatry, Psychology and Law*, 2020; 27(3):386-396, 11 June 2020, www.ncbi.nlm.nih.gov/pmc/articles/PMC7534260/

References

Lenhart, Amanda, Ybarra, Michele and Price-Feeney, Myeshia, 'Nonconsensual Image Sharing: One in 25 Americans has been a Victim of "Revenge Porn"', Data & Society Research Institute, 13 December 2016, datasociety.net/pubs/oh/Nonconsensual_Image_Sharing_2016.pdf

Young, Sarah, 'One in seven young women receive revenge porn threats, finds Refuge survey', the *Independent*, 6 July 2020, www.independent.cMI-laws#:~:text=According%20to%20a%20survey%20of,posted%20online%20without%20their%20consent

Janjigian, Lori, 'Nearly 10 million Americans are victims of revenge porn, study finds', *Business Insider*, 13 December 2016, www.businessinsider.com/revenge-porn-study-nearly-10-million-americans-are-victims-2016-12?r=US&IR=T

Online Safety Act 2023, UK Public General Acts, https://www.legislation.gov.uk/ukpga/2023/50/enacted

Cicurel, Deborah, 'From Kim Kardashian to Jennifer Lawrence, the celebrities who have taken a stand against slut-shaming', *Stylist*, 2016, www.stylist.co.uk/people/the-celebrities-who-have-taken-a-stand-against-slut-shaming-sex-nudity-speaking-out-kim-kardashian-lena-dunham-jennifer-lawrence/27354

Miller, Julie, 'Jennifer Lawrence Describes the Emotional Roller Coaster of Her Celebrity', *Vanity Fair*, 2 October 2015, www.vanityfair.com/hollywood/2015/10/jennifer-lawrence-celebrity

Suler, John, 'The Online Disinhibition Effect', *Cyberpsychology & Behavior*, 7(3):326-326, 28 July 2004, www.liebertpub.com/doi/10.1089/1094931041291295

Morrish, Lydia, 'Instagram Is Removing Sex-Positive Accounts Without Warning', *WIRED*, 29 June 2023, https://www.wired.co.uk/article/instagram-removing-sex-positive-accounts-without-warning

Hurst, Brogan-Leigh, 'Pamela Anderson and Tommy Lee's wildest moments – and immediate reaction to sex tape leak,', *Daily Mirror*, 29 January 2022, https://www.mirror.co.uk/3am/celebrity-news/pamela-anderson-tommy-lees-wildest-26052998

Sinha, Charu, 'Paris Hilton Says Nonconsensual Sex Tape Release Gave Her PTSD', *The Cut*, 18 April 2021, www.thecut.com/2021/04/paris-hilton-says-release-of-2004-sex-tape-gave-her-ptsd.html

Sisley, Dominique, 'A Kim Kardashian mural has been defaced with the word "SLUT"', *Dazed*, 15 March 2016, www.dazeddigital.com/artsandculture/article/30382/1/a-kim-kardashian-mural-has-been-defaced-slut-australia

References

'Who is Andrew Tate? One of the most googled person in world', *Economic Times*, 25 October 2022, https://economictimes. indiatimes.com/news/international/us/who-is-andrew-tate-one-of-the-zmost-googled-person-in-the-world/articleshow/94421929. cms?from=md

YouGov, Survey on Andrew Tate, https://today.yougov.com/topics/entertainment/explore/influencer/Andrew_Tate

Kelly, Emma, 'Big Brother's Andrew Tate says women should "bear responsibility" for being raped in vile tweets', the *Metro*, 19 October 2017, https://metro.co.uk/2017/10/19/big-brothers-andrew-tate-says-women-should-bear-responsibility-for-being-raped-in-vile-tweets-7011756/#:~:text=But%20some.-,',you%20must%20bare%20some%20responsibility

Your Mom's House Studios, *YouTube*, Your Mom's House Podcast w/ Andrew Tate - Ep.636, 2022, https://www.youtube.com/watch?v=vsp69jYlYsg

YouTube, ' "Cheating For a Woman is MUCH WORSE Than It Is For A Man." - Andrew Tate,' https://www.youtube.com/watch?v=USn2P_XOp9I

Lawson, Robert, '*Language and Mediated Masculinities: Cultures, Contexts, Constraints*' OUP USA, 2023

Gallagher, Sophie, 'I'm 32 years old – so why am I and all my friends so worried about fertility?' iNews, 26 July 2023, https://inews.co.uk/inews-lifestyle/fertility-anxious-millennials-why-worried-pregnancy-2503743

Chapter Five: Boys will be boys, but girls will be sluts

European Commission, 2022, "The gender pay gap situation in the EU" – https://commission.europa.eu/strategy-and-policy/policies/justice-and-fundamental-rights/gender-equality/equal-pay/gender-pay-gap-situation-eu_en

Ahn, Ashley, 'Feminists are protesting against the wave of anti-feminism that's swept South Korea', NPR, 3 December 2022, https://www.npr.org/2022/12/03/1135162927/women-feminism-south-korea-sexism-protest-haeil-yoon

Herbenick, Debby, 'Women's Experiences With Genital Touching, Sexual Pleasure, and Orgasm: Results From a U.S. Probability Sample of Women Ages 18 to 94', *Journal of Sex & Marital Therapy*, 9 August 2017

Kontula, Osmo & Miettinen, Anneli, 'Determinants of female sexual orgasms', *Socioaffective Neuroscience & Psychology Volume* 6, 25 October 2016, https://www.ncbi.nlm.nih.gov/pmc/articles/PMC5087699/#:~:text=Previous%20studies%20have%20provided%20consistent,2001%3B%20Kontula%2C%202009).

286

References

Bell, Robin, 'Homosexual Men and Women', *MBJ 1999;318:452*, 13 Feb 1999, https://www.ncbi.nlm.nih.gov/pmc/articles/PMC11 14912/

Brewer, Benjamin J., 'The Impact of Sexual Orientation on Sexuality and Sexual Practices in North American Medical Students', *The Journal of Sexual Medicine Volume 7 Issue 7*, July 2010, https://www.ncbi.nlm.nih.gov/pmc/articles/PMC3607668/

Herbenick, D. et al., 'Sexual behavior in the United States: results from a national probability sample of men and women ages 14–94', *The Journal of Sexual Medicine*, Suppl. 5:255-65, October 2010, doi: 10.1111/j.1743-6109.2010.02012.x.

Koichi Nakajima, Koichi Nagao, Toshihiro Tai, Hideyuki Kobayashi, Hiroshi Hara, Kazukiyo Miura & Nobuhisa Ishii, 'Duration of sexual intercourse related to satisfaction: survey of Japanese married couples', *Reproductive Medicine and Biology Volume 9, Issue 3*, 9 September 2010 https://www.ncbi.nlm.nih.gov/pmc/articles/PMC5904652/

Yumi Ozaki, Koichi Nagao, Rieko Saigo, Toshihiro Tai, Norie Tanaka, Hideyuki Kobayashi, Koichi Nakajima & Yoshimitsu Takahashi, 'Sexual Problems among Japanese Women: Data from an Online Helpline', *Sexual Medicine Volume 3 Issue 4*, 3 December 2015, https://www.ncbi.nlm.nih.gov/pmc/articles/PMC 4721042/

Kirstin R. Mitchell, Catherine H. Mercer,Philip Prah, Soazig Clifton, Clare Tanton, Kaye Wellings & Andrew Copas, 'Why Do Men Report More Opposite-Sex Sexual Partners Than Women? Analysis of the Gender Discrepancy in a British National Probability Survey', *The Journal of Sex Research* Volume 56, 25 July 2018, https://www.ncbi.nlm.nih.gov/pmc/articles/PMC6326215/

Booth, James, 'The Real Reason Men Lie About the Number of Women They've Slept With', *DMarge*, 8 January 2022, www.dmarge.com/men-lie-sexual-partners

Vrangalova, Zhana, 'Can Renouncing Promiscuity Help You Find Monogamous Love?', *Psychology Today*, 11 April 2016, www.psychologytoday.com/gb/blog/strictly-casual/201604/can-renouncing-promiscuity-help-you-find-monogamous-love

'Why men say they've had more lifetime sexual partners than women', *ScienceDaily*, 26 July 2018, www.sciencedaily.com/releases/2018/07/180726161251.htm

Gurney, Dr Karen, *Mind The Gap: The Truth About Desire and How to Futureproof Your Sex Life*, Headline Home, 2020

Blair, Olivia, 'Taylor Swift claims she was the "national lightning rod for slut-shaming" during her early twenties', *Independent*, 19 April2016,www.independent.co.uk/news/people/taylor-swift-claims-she-was-the-national-lighting-rod-for-slutshaming-during-her-early-twenties-a6991806.html

Charman, Helen, 'Slut-Shaming, Taylor Swift and Female Sexuality', *Huffington Post*, 26 February 2013, www.huffingtonpost.co.uk/helen-charman/slutshaming-taylor-swift_b_2757918.html

Wood, Wendy & Eagly, Alice, 'Biosocial Construction of Sex Differences and Similarities in Behaviour', in Olson, J. and Zanna, M. P. (Eds.), *Advances in Experimental Social Psychology*, 46:55-123, Elsevier, 2012, www.researchgate.net/publication/279959407_Biosocial_Construction_of_Sex_Differences_and_Similarities_in_Behavior

Chapter Six: Slutshaming across the class divide

Ashley, B., Does class impact the way we have sex?, *The Face*, 9 June 2022, theface.com/life/how-does-class-affect-how-we-have-sex

Fahs, Breanne, 'Nine Ways That Capitalism is Ruining Sex', *Boston Review*, 5 August 2022, www.bostonreview.net/articles/nine-ways-that-capitalism-is-ruining-sex/

Ghodsee, Kristen, *Why Women Have Better Sex Under Socialism*, Bodley Head, 2018

Palmer, M., Clarke, L., Ploubidis, G. & Wellings, K., 'Prevalence and correlates of "sexual competence" at first heterosexual intercourse among young people in Britain', *British Medical Journal*, 14 January 2019, srh.bmj.com/content/familyplanning/45/2/127.full.pdf

Enright, Mairead, 'The Victorian Social Purity Movement; a Noble Pursuit or "Morality Crusade"?' University of Birmingham, Birmingham Blogs, 20 March 2018, blog.bham.ac.uk/legalherstory/2018/03/20/the-victorian-social-purity-movement-a-noble-pursuit-or-morality-crusade/

'High-Status Co-Eds Use "Slut Discourse" to Assert Class Advantage', *ASA News*, 27 May 2014, www.newswise.com/articles/high-status-co-eds-use-slut-discourse-to-assert-class-advantage

Spencer, Bettina, 'Sexualization, The Impact of Class and Sexuality-Based Stereotyping on Rape Blame', *Media, & Society*, 25 April 2016

Phipps, A., 'Rape and Respectability: Ideas about Sexual Violence and Social Class', *SAGE Publications*, in *Sociology*, 43(4), 667–683, 1 August 2009, journals.sagepub.com/doi/10.1177/0038038509105414

Grossman, J., Jenkins, L. & Richer, A., 'Parents' Perspectives on Family Sexuality Communication from Middle School to High

References

School', *International Journal of Environmental Research and Public Health*, 15(1):107, January 2018, www.ncbi.nlm.nih.gov/pmc/articles/PMC5800206/

Reiss, Ira L., 'Social Class and Premarital Sexual Permissiveness: A Re-Examination', *American Sociological Review,* Vol. 30, No. 5, October 1965, www.jstor.org/stable/2091142

Clarke, D., 'Opinion on relationships/marriages to different social classes in Great Britain 2017', *Statista,* 18 September 2018, www.statista.com/statistics/778782/opinion-on-different-social-class-relationships-great-britain/

Bergström, Marie, *The New Laws of Love: Online Dating and the Privatization of Intimacy,* Polity, 2021

Phillips, Melanie, 'Why Shannon is one more victim of the folly of "lifestyle choice"', *Daily Mail,* 17 March 2008, www.dailymail.co.uk/columnists/article-536528/Why-Shannon-victim-folly-lifestyle-choice.html

Jones, Owen, *Chavs: The Demonization of the Working Class,* Verso Books, 2012

Atwood, Margaret, *The Handmaid's Tale,* Houghton Mifflin Harcourt, 1986

Chapter Seven: How racism and slutshaming intertwine

Natarajan, M. et al., 'Decolonizing Purity Culture: Gendered Racism and White Idealization in Evangelical Christianity', *Psychology of Women Quarterly*, 46(3), 5 May 2022, journals.sagepub.com/doi/full/10.1177/03616843221091116

Lim, J. & Fanghanel, A., ' "Hijabs, Hoodies and Hotpants"; negotiating the "Slut" in SlutWalk', *Geoforum*, 23 April 2013, www.sciencedirect.com/science/article/abs/pii/S0016718513001139

Calamity Andy, 'What makes you a SLUT?', YouTube, 2017, www.youtube.com/watch?v=hsGRUUHosq4&t=135s

Brinkhurst-Cuff, C., 'Amber Rose Is Not Who You Think She Is', *The New York Times*, 1 July 2022, www.nytimes.com/2022/06/30/special-series/amber-rose-slutwalk.html

von Unwerth, Ellen (photographer), 'Minaj à Trois', *Paper*, 15 November 2017, www.papermag.com/break-the-internet-nicki-minaj-sexy-full-story#rebelltitem26

Bailey, Moya, Crunk Feminist Collective blog, 2010

References

Wilson, Dominique R. 'The Sexual Exploitation of Black Women from the Years 1619 – 2020', *Journal of Race, Gender, & Ethnicity*, 10(1), 2021, digitalcommons.tourolaw.edu/jrge/vol10/iss1/13/

Morris, Natalie, *Mixed/Other: Explorations of Multiraciality in Modern Britain*, Trapeze, 2021

Loury, Glenn C., 'An American Tragedy: The legacy of slavery lingers in our cities' ghettos', 1 March 1998, https://www.brookings.edu/articles/an-american-tragedy-the-legacy-of-slavery-lingers-in-our-cities-ghettos/

Smith, Andrea, 'Not an Indian Tradition: The Sexual Colonisation of Native Peoples', VAWNet, April 2003, vawnet.org/material/not-indian-tradition-sexual-colonization-native-peoples#:~:text=Not%20an%20Indian%20Tradition%3A%20The%20Sexual%20Colonization%20of%20Native%20Peoples,-General%20Material&text=This%20paper%20analyzes%20the%20connections,the%20logic%20of%20sexual%20violence.

Epstein, Rebecca, Blake, Jamilia J. & González, Thalia, 'Girlhood Interrupted: The Erasure of Black Girls' Childhood', Center on Poverty and Inequality, Georgetown Law, 2017, genderjusticeandopportunity.georgetown.edu/wp-content/uploads/2020/06/girlhood-interrupted.pdf

Steckley, John, *White Lies About the Inuit*, University of Toronto Press, 2008

Watson, Kayleigh '"You can't really win": the hyper-scrutiny of Black women's bodies in music', *gal-dem*, 5 November 2021, gal-dem.com/hyper-scrutiny-of-black-women-in-music/

Adedeji, Jackie, More Than A Handful with Jackie, Substack, 2023, *When your wedding dress breaks the internet*. Available at: https://morethanahandful.substack.com/p/when-your-wedding-dress-breaks-the

Laskow, Sarah, 'The Racist, Slut-Shaming History of Adultery Laws', *Atlas Obscura*, 21 August 2015, www.atlasobscura.com/articles/the-racist-slutshaming-history-of-adultery-laws

Ezaydi, Shahed, *The Othered Woman: How White Feminism Harms Muslim Women*, Unbound, 2023

Mooroo, Alya, *The Greater Freedom: Life as a Middle Eastern Woman Outside the Stereotypes*, Little A, 2019

Valenti, Jessica, 'Opinion: SlutWalks and the future of feminism', *Washington Post*, 3 June 2011, www.washingtonpost.com/opinions/slutwalks-and-the-future-of-feminism/2011/06/01/AGjB9LIH_story.html

References

Black Women's Blueprint, 'An open letter from Black women to the SlutWalk', *Gender & Society*, 30(1), 19 October 2015, journals.sagepub.com/doi/10.1177/0891243215611868

Hobson, Janell, 'Should Black Women Oppose the SlutWalk? *Ms. Magazine* Blog, 28 September 2011, www.bwss.org/should-black-women-oppose-the-slutwalk-ms-magazine-blog-by-janelle/

Carr, Joetta, L., 'The SlutWalk Movement: A Study in Transnational Feminist Activism', *Journal of Feminist Scholarship*, 4(4), Spring 2013, digitalcommons.uri.edu/cgi/viewcontent.cgi?article=1071&context=jfs

Mendes, Kaitlynn, *SlutWalk: Feminism, Activism and Media*, Palgrave Macmillan, 2015

Chapter Eight: Slutshaming and the queer community

Dodge, Brian et al., 'From Bias to Bisexual Health Disparities: Attitudes toward Bisexual Men and Women in the United States', *LGBT Health*, 1(4):309–318, 26 October 2016, pubmed.ncbi.nlm.nih.gov/25568885/

Bisexual women with straight male partners least likely to be out, study finds (2021) *NBCNews.com*, https://www.nbcnews.com/

feature/nbc-out/bisexual-women-straight-male-partners-least-likely-be-out-study-n1259770

Hinge reveals the top queer dating trends of 2023 in first LGBTQIA+ dating report (no date) *Hinge*. Available at: https://hinge.co/press/2023-DATE-report (Accessed: 02 February 2024).

'Current Trends Mortality Attributable to HIV Infection/AIDS – United States 1981-1990', *Centers for Disease Control and Prevention, Morbidity and Mortality Weekly Report*, 40(3):41-44, 25 January 1991, www.cdc.gov/mmwr/preview/mmwrhtml/00001880.htm#:~:text=From%201981%20through%201990%2C%20100%2C777,deaths%20were%20reported%20during%201990.

www.hiv.gov/hiv-basics/overview/history/hiv-and-aids-timeline/

Brief Timeline of AIDS, FACT LV, https://www.factlv.org/timeline.htm

HIV, World Health Organization, 2023, https://www.who.int/data/gho/data/themes/hiv-aids.

AIDS: Homophobic and moralistic images of 1980s still haunt our view of HIV – that must change', *The Conversation*. https://theconversation.com/aids-homophobic-and-moralistic-images-of-1980s-still-haunt-our-view-of-hiv-that-must-change-106580

References

Kershaw, Hannah, 'Remembering and thinking critically about the "Don't Die of Ignorance" campaign', 20 May 2018, London School of Hygiene & Tropical Medicine, placingthepublic.lshtm. ac.uk/2018/05/20/remembering-the-dont-die-of-ignorance-campaign/

'First TV ad on HIV since "tombstones" 40 years ago set to tackle attitudes stuck in the 1980s', Terrence Higgins Trust press release, 16 October 2023, www.tht.org.uk/news/first-tv-ad-hiv-tombstones-40-years-ago-set-tackle-attitudes-stuck-1980s

Spieldenner, Andrew, 'PrEP Whores and HIV Prevention: The Queer Communication of HIV Pre-Exposure Prophylaxis (PrEP)', *Journal of Homosexuality*, 63(12):1685-1697, May 2016, pubmed. ncbi.nlm.nih.gov/26930025/

Dodds, J.P. *et al.* 'Men who have sex with men: A comparison of a probability sample survey and a community based study', *Sexually Transmitted Infections Volume 82* ', Feburary 2006, https://www. ncbi.nlm.nih.gov/pmc/articles/PMC2563827/

Dubov, A. *et al.* 'Stigma and shame experiences by MSM who take Prep for HIV Prevention: A Qualitative Study', *American Journal of Men's Health, Volume 12,* November 2018, https://www.ncbi. nlm.nih.gov/pmc/articles/PMC6199453/

Soble, A. 'Homosexuality: The Nature and Harm Arguments', *The Philosophy of Sex: Contemporary Readings*, 2002

Reddish, David, 'Slut shaming of men on prep is still happening at a ridiculous rate, study finds', *Queerty*, 25 October 2018, https://www.queerty.com/slut-shaming-men-prep-still-happening-ridiculous-rate-study-finds-20181025

Wardle, L.D. (2003) *Marriage and same-sex unions: A debate.* Westport, CT: Praeger.

National LGBT survey: Summary report – GOV.UK, 2018, https://assets.publishing.service.gov.uk/media/5b3cb6b6ed915d39fd5f14df/GEO-LGBT-Survey-Report.pdf

Transgender hate (2022), Stop Hate UK, https://www.stophateuk.org/about-hate-crime/transgender-hate/

Kelly, Cait, 'Our lives are under attack': One in two Trans Australians have experienced hate, report reveals' *Guardian*, 29 August 2023, https://www.theguardian.com/society/2023/aug/29/our-lives-are-under-attack-one-in-two-trans-australians-have-experienced-hate-report-reveals

O'Neill, Brendan, 'Bring back kink-shaming', *Spiked*, 13 February 2023, www.spiked-online.com/2023/02/13/bring-back-kink-shaming/

References

McDavitt, Bryce & Mutchler, Matt, ' "Dude, You're Such a Slut!" Barriers and Facilitators of Sexual Communication Among Young Gay Men and Their Best Friends', *Journal of Adolescent Research*, 29(4):464–498, July 2014, www.researchgate.net/publication/ 268786927_Dude_You%27re_Such_a_Slut_Barriers_and_ Facilitators_of_Sexual_Communication_Among_Young_Gay_ Men_and_Their_Best_Friends

Chapter Nine: The true consequences of slutshaming

Feldmen, H.A., Goldstein, I, Hatzichristou, D.G., Krane, R.J., McKinlay, J.B., 'Impotence and its medical and psychosocial correlates: results of the Massachusetts Male Aging Study,', *National Library of Medicine*, 15 January 1994 https://pubmed.ncbi.nlm.nih. gov/8254833/

'What are the causes of vaginismus?', The Vaginismus Center, www. vaginismus-center.com/en/causes-of-vaginismus#:~:text= 90%25%20of%20all%20vaginismus%20cases%20are%20due% 20to%20psychological%20causes.&text=The%20problem% 20resides%20in%20the,been%20engraved%20in%20the%20 subconscious.

'Erectile Dysfunction', Cleveland Clinic, my.clevelandclinic.org/ health/diseases/10035-erectile-dysfunction

Engle, Gigi, 'How growing up in purity culture impacts sex', *Mashable*, 3 August 2023, mashable.com/article/purity-culture-impact-sex

Mandal, Dr Ananya, 'Types of Sexual Dysfunction', *Medical News Today*, 15 January 2019, www.news-medical.net/health/Types-of-Sexual-Dysfunction.aspx

'Redefining life-long benefits of sexual health – WHO', World Health Organization, 11 February 2022, news.un.org/en/story/2022/02/1111862

Haque, Omar Sultan & Waytz, Adam, 'Dehumanization in Medicine: Causes, Solutions, and Functions', *Perspectives on Psychological Science*, 7(2):176–186, March 2012, pubmed.ncbi.nlm.nih.gov/26168442/

Kiderra, Inga, 'When a Doctor's Visit Is a Guilt Trip,' San Diego University, 16 January 2014, today.ucsd.edu/story/when_a_doctors_visit_is_a_guilt_trip#:~:text=%E2%80%9CIf%20you%20perceive%20your%20doctor,more%20often%20than%20men%20did.

Rastrelli, Giulia & Maggi, Mario, 'Erectile dysfunction in fit and healthy young men: psychological or pathological?', *Translational Andrology and Urology*, 6(1):79–90, February 2017, www.ncbi.nlm.nih.gov/pmc/articles/PMC5313296/

References

'Roe v. Wade Summary', Britannica, 6 December 2023, www.britannica.com/event/Roe-v-Wade

'The World's Abortion Laws, Center for Reproductive Rights, 2023, reproductiverights.org/maps/worlds-abortion-laws/

'European Abortion Laws – A Comparative Overview', Center for Reproductive Rights, reproductiverights.org/wp-content/uploads/2020/12/European-abortion-law-a-comparative-review.pdf

Thomas, Tobi, 'Outrage at jail sentence for woman who took abortion pills later than UK limit', *Guardian*, 12 June 2023, www.theguardian.com/world/2023/jun/12/woman-in-uk-jailed-for-28-months-over-taking-abortion-pills-after-legal-time-limit

Offences Against the Person Act 1861, Gov UK, www.legislation.gov.uk/ukpga/Vict/24-25/100/contents

Abortion Services in Northern Ireland Northern Ireland Direct, www.nidirect.gov.uk/articles/abortion-services#:~:text=BPAS%20is%20the%20only%20access,in%20Northern%20Ireland%20offer%20abortion.

Hopkins Tanne, Janice 'Problems with contraception play big part in unplanned pregnancies, study says" *National Library of Medicine*, 17 May 2008,

Centers for Disease Control and Prevention, 'Unintended Pregnancy', March 2023, https://www.ncbi.nlm.nih.gov/pmc/articles/PMC2386600/

https://www.cdc.gov/reproductivehealth/contraception/unintendedpregnancy/index.htm#:~:text=The%20concept%20of%20unintended%20pregnancy,using%20it%20consistently%20or%20correctly.

Morgan, Lucy, 'Rape convictions are at an all-time low – is it time we ditched juries in rape trials?', *Glamour UK*, 5 June 2023, www.glamourmagazine.co.uk/article/juries-rape-trials-law-commission

Syal, Rajeev, 'Nearly 70% of rape victims drop out of investigations in England and Wales', *Guardian*, 30 May 2023, www.theguardian.com/society/2023/may/30/nearly-70-of-victims-drop-out-of-investigations-in-england-and-wales

O'Grady, Sarah, 'Nearly 70 pc of rape claims are dropped by victims due to trauma and low conviction rates', *Express*, 31 May 2023, www.express.co.uk/news/uk/1776184/rape-claims-dropped-victims

Van Dam, Andrew, 'Less than 1% of rapes lead to felony convictions. At least 89% of victims face emotional and physical consequences.', *Washington Post*, 6 October 2018, www.washingtonpost.com/business/2018/10/06/less-than-percent-

References

rapes-lead-felony-convictions-least-percent-victims-face-emotional-physical-consequences/

Pullar, Jess, 'In Australia, Just 1.5% Of Sexual Assaults Result In A Conviction—The Consequences Cannot Be Overstated', *Marie Claire*, 12 October 2021, www.marieclaire.com.au/latest-news/criminal-convictions-sexual-violence-australia/#:~:text=In%20Australia%2C%20Just%201.5%25%20Of,goes%20beyond%20any%20court%20room

Warren-Lister, Megan, 'Victims are being failed by police officers who *still* believe in rape myths', *Glamour UK*, 6 June 2023, www.glamourmagazine.co.uk/victims-failed-police-officers-rape-myths

Roche, Barry & Pollak, Sorcha, ' "Victim blaming" criticised at protests over lawyer's thong comments', *Irish Times*, 14 November 2023, www.irishtimes.com/news/ireland/irish-news/victim-blaming-criticised-at-protests-over-lawyer-s-thong-comments-1.3697663

Osbourne-Crowley, Lucia, *My Body Keeps Your Secrets*, The Indigo Press, 2021

'EU calls for end of violence against women', European Commission, 24 November 2023, https://commission.europa.eu/news/eu-calls-end-violence-against-women-2023-11-24_en#:~:text=One%20

in%20three%20women%20both,come%20from%20the%20
employment%20context.

'What is consent?', Crown Prosecution service, Gov UK, www.
cps.gov.uk/sites/default/files/documents/publications/what_is_
consent_v2.pdf

Batha, Emma, 'Rape conviction rates rise 75% in Sweden after
change in the law', *Reuters*, 22 June 2020, www.reuters.com/
article/idUSKBN23T2R2/#:~:text=LONDON%20(Thomson%
20Reuters%20Foundation)%20%2D,2018%20to%20sex%20
without%20consent.

'Number of rape and sexual assault cases recorded by police in
Germany 2010-2022', *Statista*, September 2023, www.statista.
com/statistics/1107371/rape-and-sexual-assault-cases-number-
police-record-germany/#:~:text=Increased%20crime%20
clearance%20rate&text=In%20recent%20years%2C%20
the%20German,in%20the%20number%20of%20cases.

Hampton, Andrew, *Working with Boys: Creating Cultures of
Mutual Respect in Schools*, Routledge, 2023

Wu Zetian is Taking Apart Slut Shaming in Chinese Culture,
Polyester Zine, https://www.polyesterzine.com/features/wu-zetian-
is-taking-apart-slut-shaming-in-chinese-culture

Acknowledgements

To my brilliant agent, Florence Rees from AM Heath, who has shared so much wisdom and kindness, been so supportive of my career, and insisted 'There are no stupid questions,' when I was definitely asking some stupid questions.

To my wonderful editor, Phoebe Jascourt. From our very first meeting about *Sluts*, it was so clear that we shared the same vision and were on the same mission for this book. To have my manuscript in such safe hands for my debut book meant so much to me, as did your ability to take my chaotic phone calls with 63525272 ideas on the brain and help me turn them into action. Your support has been wonderful, as has the support of my other brilliant editors: Charlotte Moore, Amina Youssef and Pippa Shaw. It's been so empowering to work with a group of such intelligent and creative women.

To Rachel Thompson, fellow author and my editor at Mashable, who gave me so much flexibility and understanding around my features writing while I wrote this book and also put up with many 'Is it normal to feel this way??!!' messages at various points throughout the process.

To all my incredible, intelligent and hot friends, but especially Lauren Du Bignon, Molly Jameson, Serena Dicks, Ellora Sutton, Lucy Cupit, Natasha O'Neill, Katie Baskerville, Goblin, Becki Crossley and Charlotte Cooper for being such supportive friends throughout my writing process. Thank you so much for being so gassed to hear about the book deal and cheerleading me along the way (sometimes literally). Thanks for bearing with me when I had to go MIA to write the book too. We can finally go to the pub now.

To Stevie, my dog. I know you can't read, but I've appreciated every cuddle throughout this year and all the times you sat on my feet while I wrote.

To Harry, my husband, who has given me so much love and support so I could give everything to this book and showed so much excitement for its release that you've basically become a walking advert for it. Thank you for spell-checking my work, for calming me back down when I woke up at three a.m. whispering 'What if I can't write the book?', while you were trying to sleep and for making sure I remembered to celebrate the wins, as well as work hard. You're the best.

Acknowledgements

Most of all, I want to thank my family. Especially my mum, my nan and grandad, my uncles Nathan and Jimmy and my aunties Rachael and Mandy. Thanks for standing by your incredibly stubborn daughter/grandaughter/niece who refused to do anything else for a job except writing. Thanks for never saying it was a pipe dream but also being realistic about how hard I'd have to work, and for making me do it. Thank you for being so excited about the book even though this is probably not the book you had envisioned when I went on (and on) about wanting to be an author when I was a kid. Thank you for checking in on me throughout the process, and providing many cups of coffee when I walked through your door unannounced, tearing my hair out over writer's block.

My mum also deserves an extra special thanks for providing SO much information about witches and Tudors (you're obsessed!) and having literal hours-long feminist discussions with me, which shaped this book. Almost every single chapter started with a conversation with you, so the book literally wouldn't exist without you. And if it wasn't for your determination to raise me as confident, open and unafraid wherever possible, I don't think I'd have my career either. The world needs more mums like you.